Finney's Finds

The Bay Area's Consumer Watchdog Shows You Where to Find Funky, Fun, & Cheap Deals

Michael Finney

WIRES&LIGHTS
PUBLISHING

Finney's Finds
The Bay Area's Consumer Watchdog Shows You
Where to Find Funky, Fun, and Cheap Deals
©2013 Michael Finney

Wires & Lights
Michael@WiresandLightsPublishing.com
www.finneysfinds.com

Cover and book design:
Michael Brechner/Cypress House

Photos of Michael Finney copyright
© Jonathan Sprague: www.jonathansprague.com

Shopping bags on front cover
© iStockphoto.com/kyoshino

Publisher's Cataloging-in-Publication Data
Finney, Michael, 1956-
   Finney's finds : the Bay Area's consumer watchdog shows you
where to find funky, fun, and cheap deals / Michael Finney. -- 1st
ed. -- Alamo, Calif. : Wires & Lights, c2013.
     p. ; cm.
ISBN: 978-0-9882860-0-9
eBook ISBN: 978-0-9882860-1-6
     Included index.
     Summary: An indispensible guide to shopping in the San Francisco Bay Area. The author has found the stores with the best prices, largest selection and most unique merchandise.--Publisher.
     1. Shopping--California--San Francisco Bay Area--Guidebooks.
2. Stores, Retail--California--San Francisco Bay Area--Guidebooks.
3. Specialty stores--California--San Francisco Bay Area--Guidebooks. 4. Discount houses (Retail trade)--California--San Francisco Bay Area--Guidebooks. 5. San Francisco Bay Area (Calif.)--Guidebooks. 6. Consumer education. I. Title.
     TX336.5.C22 S445 2013   2012948351
640.73/0979461--dc23 1210

Printed in the United States of America

2 4 6 8 9 7 5 3 1
First edition

Finney's
Finds

For my mother, Nancy Finney —
The best shopper the Bay Area
has ever known.

About the Author

Michael Finney has received many awards in broadcast journalism, including honors from several press clubs, the National Academy of Television Arts and Sciences, the Radio-Television News Directors Association, and the Associated Press. Community groups such as Consumer Action, the Foundation for Taxpayer and Consumer Rights, and the National Association of Consumer Advocates have also honored his work. Michael's *7 On Your Side* consumer reports can be seen nightly on *ABC 7 News* in San Francisco. His highly rated talk show is heard on KGO Radio each Saturday afternoon between 1:00 and 4:00. His first book, *Michael Finney's Consumer Confidential,* was a bestseller.

Contents

Introduction

How to Use This Book

Shopping should be like travel. The destination, or item you buy, should not be your only goal — it's the process that's important. Like travel, shopping should be an adventure, eye opening and life affirming. Going into a store just to pick up a few things is no fun, but stalking the perfect deal — now that's worth your time and effort. Women have always understood this. That's why they shop with friends: to share the thrill of the hunt. It's why women tend to enjoy shopping, while men, who often shop alone, generally don't.

The stores listed in this book are here because they offer the best value, the best experience, and/or a unique product. National brand names are generally left out because you already know about them. There's no need for me to waste your time explaining that Wal-Mart and Target have huge selections and great prices. They do. You and I both know it.

In this book you will find a listing of the outlet malls in and around the Bay Area. I want to make sure you get in on the deals and don't overlook a good shopping center; however, I see no need to list every store in every mall. By now we all know the "usual suspects" and where they do business. They offer outstanding value but, again, you know about them. I do point out the occasional outlet-mall store, usually because they're rare enough that they could be overlooked.

Before you leave on a shopping trip, please confirm the information in this book. This economy and the Internet have teamed up to really hurt local merchants. I chose the listings in part because I believe the stores are strong enough to survive, but some might not. Others will change locations, phone numbers, or hours of operation. Also mistakes happen and there can be oversights. So it is important that you do not rely on this information alone and check with the stores personally before shopping. Prior to buying online, please call and confirm the Web address — there are lots of bad guys lurking out there.

1

Clothing and Department Stores

Baughman's Western Outfitters

Address	2029 First Street Livermore, CA 94554
Phone	925 447-5767
Website	www.Baughmans.com
Days & hours of operation	Mon.–Tues. 10 AM–6 PM Wed. 10 AM–7 PM Thurs.–Fri. 10 AM–8 PM Sat. 10 AM–6 PM

Description

Also Christesen's Western & English Saddlery
633 Main Street • Pleasanton, CA 94566
925 846-2169

The last time I was here, shoppers wearing spurs were looking through the merchandise. Not Folsom Street chromed spurs, but actual working cowboy spurs. Man, talk about authentic — Baughman's Western Outfitters is the real deal. The store first opened in 1881 and it's still going strong in the heart of downtown Livermore. It's easy to spot with the life-sized statue of a horse out front. Baughman's sells well-known brands of Western wear, boots, and hats, including Wrangler, Pendleton, Tony Lama, and Stetson. A large room in the back is devoted to boots. There's a vast collection of Montana Silversmith Jewelry, and plenty of belts and huge buckles. There are racks of Western-cut suits and sport coats that will bring out the J. R. Ewing in anyone. Authentic — and way cool — Western-cut shirts sell for around $50, and cowboy hats, fit for any country concert, go for $25.

Golden Bear Sportswear

Address	200 Potrero Avenue San Francisco, CA 94103
Phone	415 863-6171
Website	www.goldenbearsportswear.com
Days & hours of operation	Mon.–Thurs. 9 AM–5 PM Fri. 9 AM–4 PM

Description

You go up to a deserted building on a side street. There's a button. You push it and get buzzed in. You climb a stairway to the second story, past a couple rows of desks and office workers, then into the factory store. You see racks and racks of jackets selling at huge markdowns. The smell of leather wafts through the air. There's a window on the far side of the room where you can look out onto the factory floor and watch jackets being made. Golden Bear Sportswear has been making leather jackets since 1922. The factory store offers recent styles for well below retail. The last time I was there, suede vests with stitches in a diamond pattern were selling for $75! The suede jacket President Clinton was photographed in came from Golden Bear, and I picked up one just like it for under $100. San Francisco motorcycle officers shop here, as do football stars picking up varsity jackets. Want a bomber jacket? These guys made bombers for WWII pilots. Get the real thing at 30% or maybe even 50% off. Golden Bear is family owned. I love these guys!

Gucci Outlet

Address	321 Nut Tree Road, Suite 284 Vacaville, CA 95687
Phone	707 447-0104
Website	www.gucci.com
Days & hours of operation	Mon.–Sat. 10 AM–9 PM Sun. 10 AM–6 PM

Description

There aren't many Gucci Outlets around, so this one feels pretty special. All the items you would expect for as much as 50% off, sometimes more. Men's and women's clothing, leather goods, and shoes are available. The shoes are a particularly good deal, with many sizes and current styles, if not the latest "model year." The staff is helpful and knowledgeable. Do not come here looking for a bargain on clothes; come looking for bargains on Gucci — one of the premier designers of our times.

ISDA & CO

Address	21 South Park San Francisco, CA 94107
Phone	877-947-3760
Website	www.isda-and-co.com
Days & hours of operation	Mon.–Sat. 10 AM–6 PM

Description

This store is right on South Park, the street and the park, so it's worth a stroll here just for the young urban/social media/startup vibe, a vibe that permeates the store as well. ISDA products tend to be neutral in color and European inspired. They look and feel upscale. Currently ISDA's short jacket made of lightweight crinkled material is a hit and is seen around town on stylish women. They retail for $100 and up, but here they start at 50% off. All clothes here start at half price, and work their way down in price and across this outlet's floor if they don't sell. The newer items are in the front window or nearby; those items that haven't sold move to the back of the store and their price is cut 50% again.

Jeremys

Address	Two South Park San Francisco, CA 94107
Phone	415 882-4929
Website	www.Jeremys.com
Days & hours of operation	Mon.–Wed. 11 AM–6 PM Thurs. 11 AM–8 PM Fri.–Sat. 11 AM–6 PM Sun. Noon–6 PM

Description

There's also a Berkeley location.

Walk up to this store and it feels like you're entering a well-known department store in a city you're not familiar with. Inside the pleasant storefront and entry there's a well-kept store and fixtures stocked with big-name designer brands. Now look at the prices and you'll be blown away: designer men's and women's wear at less than half the going price. Wonder how that coworker sitting next to you can dress so well on his or her salary? Jeremys — big-name designer clothes at 50%–80% off! The items are samples, seconds, damaged, and just no longer needed by the big guys. Items change daily: clothing, shoes, and accessories.

Liquid Marin

Address	709 5th Avenue San Rafael, CA 94901
Phone	415 258-9320
Website	www.liquidmarin.com
Days & hours of operation	Tues. Wed. Fri. Sat. 10 AM–6 PM Thurs. 10 AM–7 PM Sun. 11 AM–5 PM

Description

Liquid Marin is a fun place to shop, calling itself the "little department store in your community." They pack a lot of merchandise inside: clothes for the entire family, home furnishings, rugs, home accessories, bedding, and small appliances. The sign on the door reads SAVING MONEY SHOULD ALWAYS BE THIS FUN, and that's the vibe you get when you walk in. Prices are excellent because the store carries seconds and out-of-date items as well as overstocks from companies like Anthropology, Overstock.com (Overstock's overstock?), Red Envelope's returns, and items from many other retailers and companies. The inventory changes, so you get a different shopping experience each time you drop by. Liquid Marin is a good place to find inexpensive gifts for family, friends, and teachers, with many unique items selling for under $10. You can now also buy most of what you see in the store online at www.liquidmarin.com. Shipping is free if you spend $75 or more.

Loehmann's

Address	3161 Crow Canyon Place San Ramon, CA 94583
Phone	925 866-9464
Website	www.loehmanns.com
Days & hours of operation	Mon.-Sat. 9:30 AM-9:30 PM Sun. 11 AM-7 PM

Description

*There are also locations
in San Francisco and Sunnyvale.*

Loehmann's is a large clothing chain, but there are only three stores in the Bay Area, so many folks here aren't in on the deals. Designer dresses for half price or less. A recent shopping trip found a $1,250 Dolce & Gabbana "little black dress" for $499. A Calvin Klein compression tank that usually sells for $40 is $25 here. You'll find famous-makers' men's clothing at half off. Fashion jewelry is extremely cheap, and there are great deals on sunglasses. Tom Fords that retail at $450 go for $199 here; Betsey Johnson sunglasses that list at $75 are sold for $30. There are gift and luggage sections, too. Join the Insider Club and get 15% off on your birthday; you'll also receive advance notice of sales and events.

McCaulou's

Address	589 San Ramon Valley Blvd. Danville, CA 94526
Phone	925 837-0261
Website	www.mccaulous.com
Days & hours of operation	Mon.–Sat. 10 AM–6 PM Sun. 10 AM–4 PM

Description

Ten northern California locations

It's a Contra Costa thing — a secret that you should get in on! This is a regional department store that's not only surviving but growing. A local phenomenon, it's now breaking out of Contra Costa County. These stores are filled with well-priced clothes: Men's Levi's that regularly sell for $64 are $49 here. Similar deals on other items. Women's Dockers that list for $50 sell for $40 here. Major brand names are here, and sales pop up often. There are also shoes, gifts, Cal Berkeley clothing, and whatever the latest fad is — right now it's Emi-Jay Hair Ties, Phiten Energy Bracelets, and Rick Steves backpacks. Here's the best part: free gift-wrapping with purchase.

Mycra Pac Designer Wear Outlet

Address	535 Center Street Moraga, CA 94556
Phone	925 631-6878
Website	No working website found.
Days & hours of operation	Mon.–Fri. 11 AM–4 PM

Description

Mycra Pac sells all-weather coats for women, in styles and colors you don't usually see. There's a lot of detail in each design. You'll find elaborate collars and intricate stitching on some styles, and a sophisticated choice of fabrics throughout that gives this brand a quality and flair that make it unique. The coats available for sale are packed just inside the front doors. Many are last year's colors or have small defects. Because of that they sell for half price or less. A recent visit showed brightly colored rain-type coats in various lengths, regularly priced from $210–$245, selling here for $99–$119. They also had purses and totes for sale from $29–$59. Be sure to ask about their 5% discount for cash. This is the Mycra Pac HQ, so while you shop, in the background you hear staff making deals and going about the business of their business. The outlet's located in the Rheem Valley Shopping Center.

Wingtip

Address	550 Montgomery Street San Francisco, CA 94111
Phone	415 765-0993
Website	Wingtip.com
Days & hours of operation	Mon.– Sat. 10 AM – 6 PM, Sun. By appointment only

Description

This is the former On The Fly. This is what a gentleman's store is supposed to be all about — upscale but not fussy. The best of clothes, accessories, grooming supplies, home and leisure items all displayed in an upscale environment. I recently introduced a friend to Wingtip and after looking over the clothes, cufflinks, and leather goods he said, "This is everything I care about in life." It was a joke, but for a well-dressed man, not far from the truth. The prices are very good for this quality and selection, but if you know how to work it, this place is actually a bargain. There is a wingtip reward program that offers points good for future discounts of 10%. If you join the Wingtip Social Club your monthly dues are redeemable in the store dollar for dollar. Members who spending above the dues level receive a 25% discount. Throw in sale merchandise and you are living big.

Royal Robbins Outlet

Address	841 Gilman Street Berkeley, CA 94710
Phone	510 527-1961
Website	www.RoyalRobins.com
Days & hours of operation	Mon.-Sat. 10 AM–6 PM Sun. 11 AM–5 PM

Description

This is a factory outlet, and the deals can stun you: up to 80% off at times. Experienced travelers know this brand because it's built for travel. Royal Robbins has been at it for thirty years. Rugged, lightweight, and easy-care pants, shirts, and shorts are the mainstays. There are also accessories like hats, travel bags, and backpacks. Many items at the outlet sell for 30% below retail, and there are additional markdowns during sidewalk sales and specials. A recent shopping trip netted amazingly lightweight long pants, which usually sell for $55, for just $38.50. A women's V-neck knit shirt was on sale at $23. Come here for your next trip to the outback or New York City.

Bear Basics / T-Shirt Orgy

Address	2350 Telegraph Avenue Berkeley, CA 94704
Phone	510 883-9050
Website	www.Bearbasics.com
Days & hours of operation	Mon.–Sun. 11 AM–6:30 PM

Description

T-Shirt Orgy and Bear Basics share the same building, on Telegraph between Channing Way and Durant Avenue. The combined effort means more T-shirts under one roof than perhaps anywhere else on earth. They have the expected Cal wear, but oh, so much more. I'm talking about three floors of T-shirts that you could spend hours exploring. The basement is packed full of music- and rock band-themed shirts, so your favorite group is likely there. They also have Bay Area-themed shirts, shirts that make a statement, or not, and shirts that are just silly or fun. Prices are pretty good too, with many shirts in the $10–$20 range. It's mostly men and women's sizes, but there's stuff for kids, too.

Tart Outlet

Address	2304 Willow Pass Road Concord, CA 94520
Phone	925 689-1343
Website	www.tartcollections.com
Days & hours of operation	Mon.–Sat. 11 AM–7 PM Sun. Noon–6 PM

Description

This outlet features clothing from the Tart Collections line, a brand you can see celebrities wearing in magazines. It's conveniently located one block East of Concord's Todos Santos Plaza, at Colfax and Willow Pass Road. The space itself is nothing fancy, but it's a great place to find trendy tops and knit dresses at really good prices. Part of the beauty of it is its easy pricing policy. Knit tops go for $25, sundresses are $35, and full-length casual dresses/cover-ups sell for $45. You can also find jackets and coats in various lengths and styles, from wool to leather, ranging in prices from $50–$80. There's a plus-size women's section, too. Unlike many outlets, all sales are not final here. If you get an item home and change your mind, this store will allow you to exchange it.

The North Face Outlet

Address	1238 5th Street Berkeley, CA 94710
Phone	510 526-3530
Website	www.TheNorthFace.com
Days & hours of operation	Mon.–Sat. 10 AM–7 PM Sun. 11 AM–5 PM

Description

This is a real outlet store, and there aren't many like it. It doesn't look big from the outside, but step through the door and you'll be blown away by how much is in here! A friend of mine says, "I'll never shop anywhere else ever again." A bit over the top, perhaps, but I know how he feels. The store is packed with tons of parkas, ski and snowboard pants, gloves, and boots. You can choose from lots of jackets for men, women, and children in either the waterproof or the warm fleece-type varieties. The prices are spectacular! It's the same North Face quality you're used to, at less than half the price. Many items are marked down 50% just for being bought here, and during sample sales there can be additional markdowns of 20%. I found a fleece jacket that started life selling for $129 marked down to $52. A thick fleece-lined ski jacket that sells for $225 retail goes for $90 here. Little kids' snowsuits, which regularly sell for $129, were on sale for $60. Style and stock is constantly changing, so if they don't have what you want today, drop by next week or next month.

Ujena

Address	1931-A Old Middlefield Way Mountain View, CA 94043
Phone	650 938-1010
Website	www.Ujena.com
Days & hours of operation	Mon.–Fri. 10 AM–5 PM

Description

This resort-wear boutique is the Ujena factory store. All Ujena products are designed and handmade here, so you get first dibs and a perfect fit. Their collections include a huge selection of styles, from bikinis to full-coverage suits, tankinis, and swim dresses. The showroom is small, but more than 400 suits in your size are just steps away. A friendly clerk sets you up with a computer, you point out your favorite selections, and they're brought to you straight from the factory floor. If you see a suit you like but want it in a different color, no problem — they can custom make a swimsuit for you, combining any of their huge selection of styles and fabrics. Look for online specials or special sales only at the factory store. On a recent visit, a few mix-and-match tops and bottoms were on sale in solid colors for $15 each piece. The ones in bolder patterns on the sale rack were $29 each piece. The showroom had a collection of one-piece suits and bikinis in bright colors or animal prints, most priced in the $50–$60 range.

2

Bridal and Formalwear

Bride's Corral

Address	150 North L Street Livermore, CA 94550
Phone	925 455-1244
Website	www.TheBridesCorral.com
Days & hours of operation	Mon.–Tues. 10:30 AM–5 PM Wed.–Thurs. 10:30 AM–7 PM Fri.–Sat. 10:30 AM–5 PM

Description

With a name like Bride's Corral you know this is going to be an experience. It is. When you walk through the door the first thing you see is a huge display case filled with tiaras. If there's a larger collection of tiaras — outside of the Tower of London — I haven't seen it. The store has been here thirty-five years, and touts itself as being the largest bridal store in the Tri Valley. When it comes to "The Big Day," the folks here have you covered, selling bridal gowns and accessories, as well as dresses for bridesmaid, flower girl, and the mother of the bride. There's also a large selection of party dresses (good for proms), well priced between $40 and $200. Bridal gowns range in price from $99 to more than your income and mine combined. Some of the best deals are found in sample sales that discount dresses up to 30%. They also rent tuxedos.

Glamour Closet

Address	114 Columbus Avenue San Francisco, CA 94133
Phone	415 391-1515
Website	www.GlamourCloset.com
Days & hours of operation	Tues. Wed. and Fri. 11 AM–7 PM Thurs: Noon — 8 PM Sat.–Sun. 11 AM–6 PM

Description

You'll find Glamour Closet in San Francisco's North Beach, just down the street from strip clubs and fine Italian dining. Those in the know come here for designer wedding gowns at up to 75% off retail. As the store says, "A Sample Sale Every Day!" The dresses come direct from designers, reps, and salons across the country. There are showroom and runway samples along with excess inventory. The brand names are impressive: Vera Wang, Monique Lhuillier, Carolina Herrera, Amsale, Pronovias, Enzoani, La Sposa, and others. With new stock arriving at least once a month and sometimes more, the trick to getting the best deal is to stop by often, go through the merchandise, and seize the perfect dress when you find it. The gowns are typically size 8 or 10, but can usually be sized up one size or down two. The store prides itself on offering a boutique experience, so you feel like you're shopping for the most important day of your life. No appointments are necessary.

Jessica McClintock Outlet

Address	25 15th Street San Francisco, CA 94103
Phone	415 553-8390
Website	www.JessicaMcClintock.com
Days & hours of operation	Mon.-Fri. 11 AM — 5 PM Sat.-Sun. 10 AM-5 PM

Description

My wife was wearing Jessica McClintock when we got married, so the designer holds a special spot in my heart. This outlet holds a special spot in my wallet! The deals here are amazing. Here's an example: One bridal gown, normally selling for $614, was marked down to $285. But that's just the beginning. A similar gown could show up on one of the sales racks at 40% or 70% off, which means you could walk out of the store with a wedding dress for under $100. Sweet. There's a large selection of short party dresses that would regularly sell in department stores $220; here they go for $65-$75. Floor-length prom dresses, which usually sell for $220-$300, go for $60-$80. If you're good at sewing on a button, there's a large selection of prom dresses that need minor repairs selling for $10-$15. On some I couldn't even find the defect. If you need a colorful wrap to match your dress, they have a ton of them in various colors for $5.

3

Shoe Stores

Brown Brothers

Address	848 Lincoln Avenue Alameda, CA 94501
Phone	510 865-3701
Website	No working website found.
Days & hours of operation	Mon.–Sat. 9:30 AM–6 PM Sun. 11 AM–4 PM

Description

You have to drive deep into Alameda to find this place, but it's hard to miss with its giant Popeye-type mascot logo. This is a small but well-stocked family-owned shoe store. Talk about unique in today's world! Brown Brothers has been around since 1881, selling shoes back east, in Oakland, and eventually here. If you grew up in Alameda, your parents brought you here for a good fit. The selection is excellent, and if they don't have what you want in stock, they'll order it. A friend of mine always says he likes shopping here because then his athletic shoes wouldn't be like every other pair he saw. Why? Because the shoes they sell here weren't ordered by big chain stores for a national audience. The latest Nikes are available here, including the limited editions. There are no sales at Brown Brothers — just lower prices than many of the other stores' sale prices.

DSW Designer Shoe Warehouse

Address	400 Post Street San Francisco, CA 94102
Phone	415 956-3453
Website	www.DSW.com
Days & hours of operation	Mon.–Sat. 10 AM–9 PM Sun. 10 AM–8 PM

Description

The bookstore is gone, and in its place is this shoe store, part of a large chain. Sales and markdowns are constantly occurring. It's your job to find the one that gets you the perfect shoe on the cheap. The store stocks most of the brands you would expect, and has a large selection of men and women's shoes. There are shoes for kids, too. Recent examples of the deals: Converse Jack Purcell plaid sneakers that you'd expect to go for around $60 sold for $44.94. A Taryn pump that retails at $129 was just $49. The best deals can be found on the top floor. Ride the escalator up three flights, walk to the back of the store, and you'll see shoes, arranged by size, in tall racks. Here the shoes are 50% off and more.

Johnston & Murphy Factory Store

Address	8300 Arroyo Circle (Gilroy Premium Outlets) Gilroy, CA 95020
Phone	408 848-4307
Website	www.johnstonmurphy.com
Days & hours of operation	Mon.–Sat. 9 AM–10 PM

Description

This is the only outlet-mall shoe store I'm pointing out separately from the malls. It rates a special shout-out because there are so few Johnston and Murphy's outlets — only four in California — and this is the only one in the north state. These shoes wear well, and so do the deals. Shoes start at about 20% off retail and go to 50% off and more. The men's selection isn't huge, but you'll find the dress shoe that goes with your suit without breaking your budget. The women's selection runs with the season, or slightly behind. If these guys are your style, you have to go to this store when you're in the area, just to see if they have what you want at a good price. They probably do.

Skechers USA

Address	2600 Mission Street San Francisco, CA 94110
Phone	415 401-6211
Website	www.skechers.com
Days & hours of operation	Mon.–Sat. 9 AM–8 PM Sun. 10 AM–7 PM

Description

You can't miss seeing this store: it's huge and green and seems very out of place. The phrase "drive a little, save a lot" applies here. This store is a Skechers USA Outlet; for some reason that designation is hard to find, but the deals aren't. The shoes sold in this store are much cheaper than those sold in Union Square, and depending on what you're looking for, the selection is greater, too. The staff is friendly, and they know how to help you find a deal. Most of the shoes in the store are on sale, with half price pretty easy to come by. Markdowns are available throughout the store. Hipsters who wouldn't be caught dead in the Union Square or Great Mall stores come here — that way, if they're caught, at least they're shopping in a cool neighborhood.

Stompers Boots

Address	323 10th Street San Francisco, CA 94103
Phone	415 255-6422
Website	www.stompersboots.com
Days & hours of operation	Mon.–Sat. 11 AM–6 PM Sun. 1 PM–5 PM

Description

Down the street from Costco, this store is a world away. It looks small from the outside and is even smaller inside, but they have plenty of boots. All those cool boots you see people wearing in San Francisco, they're here. If you need a boot they have it: motorcycle, engineer, harness, work, police, and cowboy. The brands are the ones you know and want: Wesco, Dehner, All American, Carolina, Frye, and more. If you can imagine a boot, they can have it custom made for you. Among the best deals I found were LaCrosse rubber boots with Vibram soles, a rugged outdoor activity boot, selling for just $65. Lace-up boots start at $129. The best deals are just past the showroom, where the shelves are filled with used and returned boots for sale — some clearly have never been worn.

4

Handbags and Luggage

Edwards Luggage

Address	3 Embarcadero Center San Francisco, CA 94111
Phone	415 981-7047
Website	www.edwardsluggage.com
Days & hours of operation	Mon.–Fri. 10 AM–7 PM Sat. 10 AM–6 PM Sun. Noon–5 PM

Description

Four bay area locations.

When you want the best in travel gear, come to Edwards. Many of the upscale names are sold here, like Tumi, Briggs & Riley, and Victorinox. If you're looking for a piece of luggage to do a specific job, they have it. Tumi is hard to find at a discount, but I've seen items here marked down as much as 25%, so shop the sales whenever possible. Along with the latest in luggage, there's a wide range of briefcases, messenger bags, wallets, and purses. The selection is outstanding, among the best you'll find with items of this quality. The well-stocked display case of writing instruments always captures my attention. The staff here is friendly, relaxed, and knowledgeable. They really know their stock, and they go out of their way to make you happy. For instance, they don't charge extra to put your initials on any bag you buy. There's also a wonderful assortment of gifts and travel items such as luggage scales and voltage adaptors.

It's A Girl Thing

Address	860 Willow St. Suite 400 San Jose, CA 95125
Phone	408 287-7288
Website	www.Itsagirlthinginc.com
Days & hours of operation	Tues.–Fri. 11:30 AM–7 PM Sat.–Sun. Noon–5 PM

Description

This little gem is tucked away in the smallish Willow Plaza shopping center, in the Willow Glen neighborhood of San Jose. It's a great place to find top-of-the-line handbags, shoes, jewelry, and accessories selling for 25% off and more. You can find brand names like Burberry, Gucci, Louis Vuitton, and Chanel, to name a few. Some items are new and others so gently worn no one would suspect you bought them at a consignment boutique. For example, a mint-condition Burberry handbag retailing for $750 sells for $575 here. They also have vintage items and accessories for men, including watches, belts, wallets, and jewelry. If you'd like to clear out your own closet, selected items are given 120 days to sell, and the split is 50/50.

Libaire Handbag Factory Store

Address	2100 5th Street Berkeley, CA 94710
Phone	510 843-9177
Website	www.Libaire.net
Days & hours of operation	Mon.-Fri. 9:30 AM-5 PM Sat. 10 AM-4:30 PM

Description

While you check out the store, you can watch as handbags, totes, and backpacks are made behind the counter. This is a true factory store — actually more factory than store. The leather is from Sweden and the manufacturing is done here. Libaire is a high-end handbag/backpack maker you've never heard of because they work for others. Their leather goods have been seen in the finest department stores. There are small handbags for $40, while the most expensive purses hover around $300. If you're looking for a purse/backpack, they have you covered with every imaginable combination of style, size, and color. The good humored and knowledgeable folks who work the counter are the folks who own the factory.

Rickshaw Bag Works Company Store

Address	904 22nd Street San Francisco, CA 94107
Phone	415 904-8368
Website	www.rickshawbags.com
Days & hours of operation	Weekdays, 10 AM–6 PM Weekends, Noon–4 PM

Description

There's a new messenger-bag company in town, and it's located in Dogpatch, the up-and-coming neighborhood off 3rd Street. The decaying look of the building makes this a great experience even before you walk in. The store isn't hard to spot: there's a rickshaw parked outside and a couple more on the showroom floor. The factory is here onsite, and the showroom is a space set off to the side. They sell all manner of Messenger bags and iPad and laptop sleeves, all made here in the factory. There are basic designs you can walk away with, and there are "one-ofs," which are the best reasons to visit here. There's also the built-to-order section where you select fabrics and styles and tell Rickshaw exactly how to make your bag. The colors are way cool. Prices range from $10 for a small sleeve to $190 for an amazingly well designed backpack.

Timbuk2

Address	506 Hayes Street San Francisco, CA 94102
Phone	415 252-9860
Website	www.Timbuk2.com
Days & hours of operation	Mon. Noon–6 PM Tues.–Fri. 11 AM–7 PM Sat. 10 AM–7 PM Sun. 11 AM–6 PM

Description

Timbuk2, in the heart of San Francisco's Hayes Valley, sells beautiful bags made mostly for people who are on the move. They have messenger bags, backpacks of all shapes and sizes, camera bags, plus shoulder bags, totes, and stylish covers meant to carry your Ipad or smartphone. These bags are different in that they're made in a wide range of colors, and you can even pick fabrics from their large collection and have one custom made. Fun, huh? Pricing varies, of course, but iPhone cases run between $25 and $29. Ipad covers go for $40, and messenger bags start around $119. You can usually find a good selection of bags in most sizes marked down 30%. Custom bags, of course, cost more. You can get one for $20 over whatever the bag would cost you off the shelf. Of course, some fabrics cost a little more, so prices can tick up, but hey — it's custom! All custom orders, by the way, are made in San Francisco. Most stock items are made overseas.

5

Optical

Optical Underground

Address	280 Sutter Street San Francisco, CA 94108 Neighborhood: Union Square
Phone	415 982-5106
Website	www.OpitcalUnderground.com
Days & hours of operation	Mon–Sat. 11 AM–7 PM Sun. Noon–5 PM

Description

Optical Underground is exactly that — underground. You enter the door at street level on Sutter, then immediately walk down a set of stairways into a fashionable showroom in the basement. Optical Underground sells frames and sunglasses made by the best, most exclusive companies, and they do it at deep, deep discounts. The owner, Lloyd Silverstein, has relationships with manufacturers going back decades and he gets first dibs on overruns, odd colors, and last year's models. A hot new Geek Eyewear frame that usually sells for $198 goes for $69 here. A pair of Gold and Wood designer glasses made with exotic African woods usually sells for $921, but sells here at $389 — nearly two thirds off! Glasses here start at 50% off and drop an additional 25% every ninety days.

Orion Telescopes & Binoculars Outlet Store

Address	89 Hangar Way Watsonville, CA 95076
Phone	800 676-1343
Website	www.telescope.com
Days & hours of operation	Mon.–Fri. 9 AM–5 PM

Description

If you want to scan the night sky or track that ship out there at sea, Orion has you covered, with everything for the amateur astronomer and nature enthusiast, from beginner to advanced, at dramatically reduced prices. This warehouse store is packed with the newest and best telescopes, binoculars, and accessories. The best deals, however, are those offered on samples, seconds, and refurbished items. An Orion GoScope 80mm Table Top Refractor Telescope that usually sells for $119 is sold as a second for $101. An Orion BT70 Premium Binocular Telescope sells for $599, but as a second it's priced at $479. Many items are available only in limited quantities, so it's first come first served!

Sunglass & Optical Warehouse

Address	3450 Kurtz Street, Suite D San Diego, CA 92110
Phone	619 291-4810
Website	www.sunglassoptical.com
Days & hours of operation	Mon.–Fri. 9 AM–7 PM Sat. 9 AM–6 PM Sun. 9 AM–5 PM

Description

Three locations in San Diego

Yes, this store is in San Diego, a long drive, but they do have some of the best prices on sunglasses in the state of California. The original store is in an industrial area tucked behind the sports arena, so it isn't exactly overwhelmed with tourists. Good — that leaves more great deals for you and me. Sunglass & Optical stocks nearly every major brand of shades, all deeply discounted. Ray-Bans sell here for about 25% less than at other stores. Sunglass & Optical Warehouse now has two other locations, but both are in San Diego. Go online and you might find a 15% discount coupon that's redeemable in their stores.

6

Jewelry

A and E Watches

Address	888 Brannan Street, Suite 218 San Francisco, CA 94103
Phone	415 437-3262
Website	www.aandewatches.com
Days & hours of operation	Mon.–Fri. 10 AM–5 PM

Description

I first met the crew here nearly two decades ago when I was searching for a discontinued Omega Sea Master watch. This was the only store that had one, and they offered it at a great price. Any watch in the world that you want, these guys have it or will find it for you. All major brands pass through here: Breitling, TAG Heuer, and Ebel to name a few. The real specialty, though, is Rolex. A&E is everything but an authorized dealer. If you're looking for a classic Rolex Submariner, you can save $1,000 buying it here. The more expensive the watch the more you can save. A new Rolex Daytona will usually set you back about $16,000 depending on the model. Buy one from A&E and you'll pay about 33% less. If you're okay with a used watch, the savings go even deeper. A&E also buys watches, so if you have a high-end watch to sell, this might be the place. A&E has an in-house service center where you can save 50%–70% on repairs. The A&E showroom is in the Gift Center & Jewelry Mart, a wholesale complex, so you'll need to call ahead and arrange to get a pass to visit the store.

Celtic Inheritance

Address	1778 Shattuck Avenue Berkeley, CA 94709
Phone	510 841-8702
Website	www.macmanusandson.com
Days & hours of operation	Tues.–Sat. 11 AM–7 PM

Description

Celtic Inheritance is also known as MacManus & Sons, so don't be confused if that name pops up. This is an amazing find: one of the world's great Celtic jewelers right here in the Bay Area. Jewelry here has Celtic heritage built in, as traditional Irish designs are made into works of wearable art. Shamrocks, the lover's knot, and various Celtic-inspired designs are used to create rings, brooches, belt buckles, and other items. The Claddagh is a time-honored Irish ring that shows two hands holding a heart, symbolizing the person who holds and governs your heart. A classic here, there are a variety of takes on this ring of friendship and love. Custom pieces are also available. The prices are amazingly low for this quality of work. Most silver pieces sell for around $100 or less; those cast in gold cost much more, depending on the going rate that day. All the jewelry is made in the shop. Additional Irish items are for sale here, too. Think in terms of traditional Irish goods.

Derco Fine Jewelers

Address	888 Brannon Street, Suite 137 San Francisco, CA 94103
Phone	415 626-7442
Website	www.Dercodiamonds.com
Days & hours of operation	Mon.–Fri. 9:30 AM–5 PM Sat. 10 AM–4 PM

Description

When you walk into this store, the glare from the diamonds nearly blinds you. There's so much here that it amazes. Mixed in with the diamonds are many colored stones. The store always seems packed, and no wonder — the service here is impeccable. The prices are well below most jewelry stores. Think in terms of 33% off retail. Derco is famous for unique designs. I know a woman who bought a ruby and diamond necklace here decades ago. She still receives compliments every time she wears it. This is a good place for young couples to buy a "starter" ring, i.e., an engagement ring with a small diamond that can be replaced later with a larger one, when they have more funds. Any diamond center stone or solitaire diamond earrings that you buy from Derco can be traded in at full purchase price for a bigger or higher-quality stone. Derco is located in the wholesale space called the Giftcenter and Jewelrymart, so you'll need to call ahead to make an appointment and get a pass.

Giraux Fine Jewelry

Address	888 Brannan Street, Suite 129 San Francisco, CA 94103
Phone	415 863-8188
Website	www.Giraux.com
Days & hours of operation	Mon/-Fri. 9:30 AM–5 PM Sat. 10 AM–3 PM

Description

Giraux has a cult-like following of customers who swear by the store and all who work here. That eases the nerves when you're getting ready to make a large purchase. In this economy, most of the jewelry sold is "must have" items, so the engagement ring, which has always been a major seller here, is now an even bigger part of the inventory. The sales staff is well versed in their products, and they know the gems and metals they sell. One of the biggest selling points is the unhurried and relaxed manner the store is famous for. You will not be up-sold here, and if they don't have what you're looking for, it simply doesn't exist. The selection is amazingly large and varied. Located in the GiftCenter and Jewelrymart, so call ahead for a pass to visit the showroom.

Simayof Diamond Cutters and Jewelers

Address	246 Powell Street (on Union Square) San Francisco, CA 94102
Phone	415 391-0152
Website	www.Simayof.com
Days & hours of operation	Mon.-Sun. 10 AM–9 PM

Description

I first met Adi Simayof nearly twenty years ago when I tried to bust him in an undercover sting. I had a beautiful young gemologist pose as a clueless woman who wanted to buy a diamond ring. Many jewelry stores treated her poorly, assuming she didn't have the wherewithal to actually buy jewelry. They tried to take advantage of her ignorance, offering her lesser stones and settings, which they claimed were much better than they really were. But not Simayof's. There, the jewelers were helpful and quick to educate her. They offered her diamonds that were exactly as represented, at prices well below what other jewelers charged. There was no hard sell, just fair prices and professionalism. The gemologist walked out amazed by Simayof's integrity. I then walked back into the store, and Adi and I have been friends since. The best way to get a deal here is to join the Simayof Rewards Program, which gives instant discounts of 30%–40% and offers a point program for repeat buyers.

Steampunk Garage

Address	Arts & Crafts Market Justin Herman Plaza
Phone	650 305-9699
Website	www.SteamPunkGarage.com
Days & hours of operation	Generally around Thursday–Sunday, midmorning to late afternoon

Description

Steampunk is an artistic/lifestyle movement that centers on an H. G. Wells and Wild West aesthetic. Think in terms of a steam-powered spaceship and you have the basic concept. The Steampunk world has many artisans, but few design and execute as well Stan Chiao and Jen Martinez. These two make pieces that speak of Steampunk but go far beyond the basic gears and watch parts. This is handmade jewelry that's not restricted to those who are into Steampunk couture. These items can be worn with many different clothing styles, and to events from street festivals to — for the daring — opera openings. The prices are amazingly good, reflecting their true street heritage and pedigree. Earrings go for about $25, bracelets $40, and necklaces around $100. Some cost more and some less. The best way to get a deal is to make your purchase at the street-artist booth. Start with one piece, then ask for a lower price for buying a second or third. I've never seen these guys discount on a single item — they may have, but I've never seen it.

Taylor & Jacobson

Address	1475 North Broadway, #490 Walnut Creek, CA 94596
Phone	925 937-9570
Website	www.Taylorjacobson.com
Days & hours of operation	Tues.–Fri. 10 AM–6 PM

Description

You find deals in the most unlikely places, and this is one of the least likely places. I first visited Taylor & Jacobson a decade ago, and I still remember the process of finding it: You go to downtown Walnut Creek to a mid-rise office building. You take an elevator up a few floors, where you knock on a door and are let in. This is not your common jewelry-buying experience. You meet with a designer and go over exactly what you want and how much you can spend. Designs are shown and discussed, changes are made, and a sketch of your piece is drawn. Once you're happy with the design, the sketch is turned into a computer rendering, and the ring you imagined is milled into wax. When the gold or platinum is eventually poured, the piece is hand finished, and in about a month the item is ready for pickup. You can use gems you already own or pick new ones from the store's collection. Special orders are available, too. If you have unused gold, bring it in for trade. This might sounds like it would all be very expensive, but it's not. Without a showroom to pay for, Taylor and Jacobson can keep the prices low. They also sell loose stones and do repairs.

7

Furniture

Berkeley Outlet

Address	711 Heinz Avenue Berkeley, CA 94710
Phone	510 549-2896
Website	www.BerkeleyOutlet.com
Days & hours of operation	Tues.–Sat. 10 AM–5 PM

Description

Moving into that city loft? Here's your go-to place for decorating. They call it used office furniture, designers call it retro, vintage, loft-style, and tank. The vintage metal collection here is huge and always changing, and this stuff will last forever. In high-end Los Angeles shops, a desk can sell for $800 or more. Here a small tank desk will set you back about $75, and a large police sergeant-type tank desk will go for $180. Bookcases and laboratory cabinets are priced from $40–$400. If you're actually setting up an office — hello, startups — Berkeley Outlet offers space planning and partitions. For those who prefer wood office furniture, that's here, too.

Brook Furniture Clearance

Address	30985 Santana Street Hayward, CA 94544
Phone	510 487-2270
Website	www.bfr.com/clearance/ sanfrancisco
Days & hours of operation	Mon.–Fri. 9 AM–5 PM

Description

All the Brook furniture that's rented in the greater Bay Area ends up here after it's returned. It's then put on display and sold for 50%–75% off retail. Though the furniture isn't new, some is so lightly used you can't tell it's not new. Some recent prices: a five-piece dining room set for $200; a sofa for $200, and a bedroom set for $400. The best way to get a deal here is to check for ads online and in local newspapers. Recent specials included 15% off for students setting up their apartments, and for seniors willing to shop on Tuesdays. There was a 10% discount coupon offered for no apparent reason. Furniture is always coming into and going out of here, so check back often if you're looking for a specific item.

California Stools, Bars and Dinettes

Address	Pleasant Hill Furniture Store 571-B Contra Costa Blvd. Pleasant Hill, CA 94523
Phone	925 825-6888
Website	www.CaStoolsBarsDinettes.com
Days & hours of operation	Mon.–Fri. 10 AM–5:30 PM Sat. 10 AM–5 PM Sun. Noon–5 PM

Description

Two additional locations in San Jose and San Carlos

Casual dining is what this store is all about. Prices on new items are reasonable, and you can buy floor samples for 30% off. This is where to go when you're trying to match a specific height, style, or intended use. It's also where to go if you don't want to feel bad because you haven't got a lot of money to spend. The staff is very sensitive to customer finances, which has helped keep them in business for thirty years. I shop here when I'm looking for stools, but they also have a huge variety of dining tables, pub sets, and home bars. Many items can be bought singly, so if you need an odd number of chairs, they can accommodate you. Check online for specials: sometimes there's not a lot there, but what's there could be just the thing you need.

Cort Furniture Clearance

Address	1240 Willow Pass Road Concord, CA 94520
Phone	925 609-9127
Website	www.cort.com/furniture-stores/ california/concord
Days & hours of operation	Mon.- Fri. 10 AM - 7 PM Sat. 10 AM - 6 PM Sun. 11 AM - 5 PM

Description

Six locations in the greater Bay Area

This is where the rental giant offloads returned rental furniture. It's lightly used, for the most part, and prices are commonly half of retail, though sometimes you can get 70% off. A high-style five-piece dining room set sells for $300, and a three-piece living room set for $400. There are also deals on new furniture, including a leather couch for $1,000. The electronics sold here tend to be nearing the end of their useful life, but at these prices they're still bargains. On a recent shopping trip, I found a DVD player for $15, and 27-inch TVs for $30. Their stock changes constantly, so dropping in occasionally can pay big dividends.

Crate & Barrel Outlet Store

Address	1785 4th Street Berkeley, CA 94710
Phone	510 528-5500
Website	www.crateandbarrel.com/outlet
Days & hours of operation	Mon.–Sun. 10 AM–7 PM

Description

You'll find the same great stuff you buy at the Union Square store, but at about half the cost. Tableware, cookware, and accessories are plentiful and are in perfect shape. The furniture, however, tends to be seconds, damaged, irregular, or on clearance. Usually, there's only one or two of each item, so if you see what you want, snatch it! To get the best deals, come often, as the stock is always changing. If you have the time and patience for it, you can collect a five-piece dining set one piece at a time, but there's no guarantee that all the pieces will be available when you drop by. Recent prices included an outdoor teak ottoman, which usually sells for $299, going for $211.65, and here, a Cuisinart Petit gas grill that retails for $120 sells for half that.

Giorgi Brothers Furniture

Address	211 Baden Ave. South San Francisco, CA 94080
Phone	650 588-4621
Website	www.GiorgiBros.com
Days & hours of operation	Mon. Wed. Fri. Sat. 9 AM–6 PM Tues. Thurs. 9 AM–8 PM Sun. 11 AM–5 PM

Description

Giorgi Brothers has been a South San Francisco institution for nearly seventy-five years. If you want the best furniture at 40%–60% off, shop here. They have relationships with nearly all manufacturers, so if you find something you like at another store or online or in a magazine, call Giorgi Brothers. They can most likely get it for you, and cheaper than anywhere else. Family owned and operated, with a fairly new showroom — it certainly seems new to those who've shopped here for years — the vibe is upscale but not stuffy. Giorgi Brothers delivers throughout the Bay Area, and if you want an item shipped out of the area, even out of state, they can handle that, too.

Hotel Furniture Liquidators

Address	775 N. 10th Street, Suite 112 San Jose, CA 95112
Phone	408 293-9765
Website	1wp.com/go/ hotelfurnitureliquidator
Days & hours of operation	Mon.–Sat. 10 AM–5 PM

Description

Shopping here is like wandering through the world's largest garage sale. The showroom even looks like a huge garage. It's packed with used furniture from hotels that were either liquidating or remodeling, brought here and sold at rock-bottom prices. They sell everything you'd find in a hotel room or suite: sleeper sofas, tables, headboards, lamps, TV stands, side tables, even remanufactured mattresses and box springs. Some items are in better condition than others, so look things over with a careful eye, but chances are they've got several of whatever you're looking for. Sleeper sofas sell for $100, leather ones for $125. Headboards, TV stands, and side tables are $45 each, and table lamps with shades go for $15. You can buy a remanufactured king mattress set for $225; twins sell for $99. Do you just love the artwork in hotel rooms? There's a ton of framed artwork here for $15 — $30. Some items are new. During a recent visit, I saw stacks of white California king duvet covers for $20. A hotel had bought way too many due to remodeling, and sold all the leftovers, still in the original packaging.

Interior Motions

Address	1490 Park Ave. Emeryville, CA 94608
Phone	510 653-6100
Website	www.InteriorMotions.com
Days & hours of operation	Mon.–Fri. 8 AM–5 PM Sat. 10 AM–4 PM

Description

If you're setting up a home office, or just love your work cubicle so much you want one in your home, Interior Motions has you covered. This warehouse store has been in the same location for over twenty-five years, selling new and pre-owned office furniture. They have a ton of desks and chairs, and, of course, cubicles. Swivel chairs sell in the $50–$75 range; high-end chairs can cost as much as $500. I found fabulous-looking wooden desks for $250. If you want to be seen as a big-time CEO, you can spend $2000. Nothing here is beat-up, so whether you're furnishing a home office or a startup, no one will know you're pinching pennies.

Macy's Union City Furniture

Address	1208 Whipple Road Union City, CA 94587-2026
Phone	510 441-8833
Website	www.macys.com
Days & hours of operation	Wed.–Sun. 11 AM–6 PM

Description

A huge warehouse in the middle of nowhere, there are no fake living rooms set up here, just great prices on returns, overstocks, and seconds. If you like shopping Macy's furniture stores, you'll love this place. Discounts start at 20%–30% off, but there are frequent markdowns. The longer an item stays on the floor the cheaper it gets. Mattresses can be spectacularly priced here — just know what you could expect to pay at retail before you shop at this warehouse and you'll be thrilled with your purchase. Sales personnel are around, but they're pretty casual, so don't get upset if they don't run over to greet you — it's not that kind of place. If you need delivery, they can handle that. It costs a few bucks and takes a while, but it beats trying to figure out how to stuff that mattress into your Fiat.

Noriega Furniture

Address	1455 Taraval Street San Francisco, CA 94116
Phone	415 564-4110
Website	www.noriegafurniture.com
Days & hours of operation	Tues. Wed. Fri. 10 AM–5:30 PM Thurs. 1 PM–9 PM Sat. 10 AM–5 PM

Description

A Sunset District favorite for over fifty years, it's worth going out of your way to shop here. The designers can access nearly any manufacturer. They have an amazing collection of Mission furniture. A recent example of pricing is the Stickley's 2012 Collector's Edition Cabinet, which retails for $1,665. Here it sells for $999. Find an item in a magazine that you've just got to have? Call Noriega Furniture, and they'll hunt it down for you at a deep discount. If you find something you like in another store, call Noriega and challenge them to beat the price. There's a good chance they'll beat it by a mile. It's that dedication to the customer that has kept this store going despite all the ups and downs of the economy.

Restoration Hardware Outlet

Address	324 Nut Tree Road Vacaville, CA 95687
Phone	707 446-3421
Website	www.restorationhardware.com
Days & hours of operation	Mon.–Sat. 10 AM–9 PM Sun. 10 AM — 6 PM

Description

There are fewer than a dozen of these Restoration Hardware Outlets nationwide, and they are the real deal. I know people who were on the verge of tears when the R. H. Outlet store in Tracy closed. They have to drive farther now, but the deals are there to be had. A friend of mine slowly and methodically collected Restoration Hardware backyard furniture one piece at a time. It took a while, but in the end she built a designer collection for about half price. None of their stuff is cheap, but you have to pay if you want the very best. Discounts range from 20% – 50% off.

Rug Depot Outlet

Address	4056 Hubbard Street Emeryville, CA 94608
Phone	510 652-3890
Website	www.rugdepotoutlet.com
Days & hours of operation	Monday–Saturday 10 AM–7 PM Sunday 11 AM–6 PM

Description

This place didn't get discovered — it got surrounded! A store that was once in an industrial area is now encircled by malls and shopping centers in the Emeryville shopping district. Rug Depot is a giant warehouse stuffed with fine carpets, with deals that are simply unobtainable at most stores. You'll find every price point here, but the mid-priced large Oriental carpets are the best deals, selling at 30%–50% off. The staff is knowledgeable, and there is no up-sale, just good, helpful customer service.

The Lampshade House

Address	120 Second Avenue San Mateo, CA 94401
Phone	650 348-1158
Website	www.thelampshadehouse.com
Days & hours of operation	Tues.–Sat. 10 AM–5 PM, but it's best to call ahead — sometimes they take unscheduled hours/days off.

Description

The Lampshade House is one crazy place. A small shop, it's jam-packed with shades in every imaginable size. With over forty years' experience in manufacturing and retailing lampshades, these guys have what you need. Every shape: cylinders, squares, rectangles, ovals, hexagons, and octagons. Every style: drums, shallow drums, bells, empires, flares, cut-corner squares, pagodas, and scallops. If they don't have what you want, they'll make it or order it for you, but really, if they haven't got what you want, you're being too picky. They also repair and customize shades and lamps. Prices range from $18 for very small shades to $200 for a huge cowboy-inspired shade.

8

Mattresses

Mancini's Sleepworld Outlet

Address	2828 Sisk Road Modesto, CA 95350
Phone	209 524-7700
Website	www.sleepworld.com
Days & hours of operation	Mon.–Fri. 10 AM–9 PM Sat.–Sun. 10 AM–7 PM

Description

Also in Santa Rosa and Gilroy

Mancini's Sleepworld offers world-class service and very good prices in each of its twenty-eight northern California stores, but some of the best deals are found in the outlet centers. These are inside regular stores, and the deals can't be beat. Floor samples and clearance mattresses and furniture are on sale here along with overstocked items. Leftovers of all types — but all first quality — end up here and at the other locations. Prices are as much as 50% off, with a king set selling for as little as $569, and futon mattresses for $98. The staff is knowledgeable and friendly.

Sleep Train Depot Outlet Store

Address	1595 Holiday Lane, Suite B Fairfield, CA 94533
Phone	707 399-9654
Website	www.sleeptrain.com
Days & hours of operation	Mon–Fri. 10 AM–9 PM Sat. 10 AM–8 PM Sun. 10 AM–7 PM

Description

Sleep Train is famous for selling the best mattresses at discount prices. Sleep Train Depot Stores take that one step further and sell floor models, demonstrators, scratched and scuffed mattresses, customer returns, freight-damaged, and discontinued models — in short, all the good stuff! Flaws that will never be noticed can save you hundreds of dollars. Clearance and floor samples from the other stores end up here, marked down at least 25%. A queen set can be had for $399. Here's a secret most don't know: you can shop at any Sleep Train store and have floor models and clearance items delivered — save on gas and tolls! Sleep Train does a great job of getting same-day delivery of its beds to regular customers; however, since the outlets have unique clearance merchandise, some might not be available for same-day delivery.

The New National Mattress Discount Center

Address	21354 Foothill Blvd. Hayward, CA 94541
Phone	510 538-1700
Website	www.Nationalmattresscenter.com
Days & hours of operation	Mon.–Fri. 9 AM–7 PM Sat. 9 AM–6 PM Sun. Noon–5 PM

Description

It's easy to pass by National Mattress Discount Center without really noticing it, but it's worth your time to take a moment. It's been in this area (at different locations) since 1934, and there are families who won't shop anywhere else. Keith has been managing the shop for years now. National Mattress has a unique business model: it's an authorized dealer for Simmons, Sealy, and Englander. Those companies and others ship directly here and have National Mattress act as an outlet store selling mismatched sets, seconds, discontinued, overstocked, and closeout models. All come with a guarantee — either a factory or store warranty. What are the prices like? As much as 50% off. On a recent visit, a king-size mismatched set was selling for $789, a Simmons queen set was going for $399, and a Sprint air twin was $169.

West Coast Clearance

Address	45 Boutwell Street San Francisco, CA 94124
Phone	415 762-8763
Website	www.WestCoastClearance.com
Days & hours of operation	By appointment and on special walk-in days

Description

Also in San Jose

This place is in San Francisco, but still way off the beaten path. It's a warehouse, a real warehouse. There are no amenities like insulation or good lighting. Still, what you find here is a true offering of mattresses and furniture closeouts, overstocks, and "others" from major companies and unknowns, all at up to 70% off. Recent examples include New Serta mattresses with factory warranty: twin $149; full $225; Cal king from $395. Then there's an eight-inch queen-size memory-foam mattress for $295. There are constant deals, but you can't just show up and get them — either call in advance to make an appointment, or wait for a special sale when they allow walk-ins.

9

Appliances

Airport Appliance Outlet Center

Address	150 Alpine Way Hayward, CA 94545
Phone	510 225-0368
Website	www.airportappliance.com
Days & hours of operation	Mon.–Fri. 9 AM–7 PM Sat. 10: AM–6 PM Sun. 11 AM–6 PM

Description

Airport Appliance is growing. A local chain, it has figured out how to play with the big boys and girls and win. There are five store locations, but this is the one that bargain hunters hone in on. Along with the newest and best, there are also last year's models and floor samples. The best deals are reserved for appliances that are scratched and dented. Some come direct from the manufacturers with minor issues, others from the chain of stores. You can find $300 discounts on appliances with dented sides that will never be seen. There are also those with major flaws that sell for as much as 80% off.

Appliance Sales and Service/The Gourmet Depot

Address	840 Folsom Street San Francisco, CA 94107
Phone	415 362-7195
Website	www.thegourmetdepotco.com
Days & hours of operation	Mon.–Fri. 8:30 AM–5:30 PM Sat. 9 AM–5 PM

Description

Appliance Sales and Service has been quietly going about its business on Folsom street for years. This company stocks more than 100,000 appliance parts, including some that it's held on to for years, just waiting for you to need one. AS&S goes so far as to buy old stock from companies going out of business. If you have an old appliance — even one that's decades old — Appliance Sales and Service likely has the part. Expert service techs can do the work, or you can do it yourself. The company is now also doing business as Gourmet Depot, selling high-end smaller appliances at deep discounts. Refurbished items are the best deals: a brand-name food processor that retails brand-new at $349 sells here for just $240.

Cherin's

Address	727 Valencia Street San Francisco, CA 94110
Phone	415 864-2111
Website	www.cherinsappliance.com
Days & hours of operation	Tues.–Fri. 9:30 AM–5:30 PM Saturday: 10 AM–5 PM

Description

Cherin's has been selling appliances in San Francisco for over a hundred years and is still family owned and run. Most of the major appliance brands are on sale here. Appliances are in an industry that offers so many discounts it's hard to keep track. Cherin's does a good job of it and posts them on a single Web page. Check there before you go to the store. Buying several appliances at the same time, such as when you're remodeling, will also get you big discounts.

Friedmans Appliance

Address	2304 Monument Blvd. Pleasant Hill, CA 94523
Phone	925 808-2950
Website	www.friedmansappliance.com
Days & hours of operation	Mon.–Fri. 10 AM–7 PM Sat.–Sun. 10 AM–5 PM

Description

Freidmans Appliance knows how to make a sale. This family-owned store offers most of the big brand names and will put together packages of appliances that come with deep discounts. One of the store's hot sellers is Electrolux. Known mainly for vacuums here in the United States, this is an important brand name in Europe. Now with the help of Kelly Ripa (the spokeswoman who manages her household with magic and Electrolux), the brand is finding a large following in the United States. Freidmans Appliance also offers discounts on discontinued and blemished merchandise, and they'll price match on new merchandise, too.

Rancho Grande Appliances

Address	2890 Bryant Street San Francisco, CA 94110
Phone	415 641-5139
Website	www.usedappliancerepairsf.com
Days & hours of operation	Mon.–Sat. 9 AM–5:30 PM

Description

On its busy corner, you can't miss this place. Used appliances are lined up on Bryant Street, then round the corner onto Cesar Chavez Street. They work as a beacon for those who want to save money. Rancho Grande refurbishes and then sells home appliances. Rather than buy a new electric range for hundreds of dollars, come here and get one for $185. Washers and driers start at $150, refrigerators $200. If you need parts or repairs, Rancho Grande can do that, too. Are you looking for a classic vintage stove from the 1940s or '50s? They usually have one or two. It's much cheaper to buy a vintage stove here than at many other places, because here it's priced like a used stove, not like an antique.

Sears Outlet

Address	680 W. Winton Avenue Hayward, CA 94545
Phone	510 265-1003
Website	www.searsoutlet.com
Days & hours of operation	Mon–Fri. 10 AM–9 PM Sat. 10 AM–9 PM Sun. 10 AM–7 PM

Description

Also in San Leandro and Milpitas

This outlet store is set up in a huge warehouse. The only thing pretty about the place is the prices. Among the best deals are the appliances. Sears is still a powerhouse in the field, and the outlet store is where you go to get the castoffs at discounts that will make a huge difference when you're remodeling your kitchen. Some examples: A Kenmore built-in side-by-side refrigerator that retails for $6,869 sells here at half price, $3,435. A Sharp 70-inch 3-D TV, regularly $3,699, sells for $1,999. Great deals on furniture, too. The items sold here are new, "like new," and reconditioned. Some will have small scratches that are easily repaired or ignored; that's why you're getting such a great deal. Discounts range from 30%–70% on mattresses, furniture, clothes, dishes, and sporting goods.

10

Outdoor Living

A Silvestri Co.

Address	2630 Bayshore Blvd. San Francisco CA 94134
Phone	415 239-5990
Website	www.asilvestri.com
Days & hours of operation	Hours vary by season.

Description

A. Silvestri has been in business in San Francisco since the 1950s. There's so much here it's hard to know where to start. More than a hundred pieces are on sale, so if you need furniture, fountains, or statues for your outdoor space, this is a great place to start. Planters, urns, sundials, and birdbaths are all on display. There's also a religious section and a collection of Asian-inspired designs. The prices are below what you'd pay at most shops, and items on sale can be drastically reduced. If you need help or education, these guys are willing to give you the time.

AW Pottery

Address	601 50th Avenue Oakland, CA 94601
Phone	510 533-3900
Website	www.awpotteryusa.com
Days & hours of operation	Mon.–Sat. 9 AM–5 PM

Description

Also in Berkeley

You can see the warehouse from I-80, but it takes a while to circle back and find the entrance. There's a fenced outside area that's packed with pottery. It can feel almost claustrophobic as you walk along paths between pots piled well above your head. Inside, the stacking goes on. AW Pottery concentrates on Asian designs and craftsmanship. Finding the right pots here will take some time, and you can expect to get dirty, as this is a warehouse, not your retail lawn and garden supply. But the prices are good, especially on the larger pots and planters.

Plant and Pottery Outlet

Address	6467C Mission Road Sunol, CA 94586
Phone	925 862-0151
Website	www.plantandpotteryoutlet.com
Days & hours of operation	9 AM–7 PM every day

Description

It certainly looks like a plant and pottery outlet. Between a country road on one side and I-680 on the other is a small metal building and a chain-link fence. Inside are pots and plants, statues and fountains. These folks import direct from Vietnam, China, Malaysia, and Mexico. The best deals are out back of the store, where chipped pottery is sold. Some is so badly damaged it's not worth buying, but other pieces, with so little damage that you have to search to find it, are marked down considerably.

The Complete Backyard

Address	1600 Duane Avenue Santa Clara, CA 95054
Phone	408 748-8100
Website	www.completebackyards.com
Days & hours of operation	Tues.–Fri. 10 AM–7 PM Sat.–Sun. 10 AM–5 PM

Description

Eclectic is how you'd describe this place, a store that specializes in outdoor kitchens, waterfalls, patio furniture, scooter repairs, and hockey equipment. Business school graduates would hurl themselves off the loading dock if they came here. When you walk into this big open warehouse, you pass the waterfalls, motorized scooters, and hockey gear before you come to the patio department. There's a good selection of outdoor furniture including a sizable collection of umbrellas and teak furniture. Barbecue islands are a major focus, and the prices are deeply discounted. The Complete Backyard says it will not be undersold, so check prices at other places and hold them to the promise. A big seller here is The Big Green Egg smoker and grill. It's the latest in outdoor cooking technology, and The Complete Backyard offers it in all five sizes and with every imaginable accessory.

11

Building Supply and Hardware

Fredericksen Hardware & Paint

Address	3029 Fillmore Street San Francisco, CA 94123
Phone	415 292-2950
Website	fredericksen.hardware@gmail.com www.fredericksenhardwareandpaint.com
Days & hours of operation	Mon.–Fri. Sat. 8 AM–7 PM Sat.–Sun. 9 AM–6 PM

Description

In business since 1896, Fredericksen is a major part of the neighborhood. They have all the hardware you'd expect of a store like this, but they do way better than that. Fredericksen stocks all the vintage items that are still used every day in homes in this part of the city: drawer pulls, window latches, and doorknobs to name a few. In most areas you'd have to go online and pay a fortune at a store specializing in renovations; here they cost a couple bucks. This store has saved me a fortune over the years. The department managers order their own stock from distributors, so they're empowered to make deals and can answer your questions. Kitchen supplies are sold here, too. About six years ago they opened a paint annex next door.

Ohmega Salvage

Address	2400–2407 San Pablo Ave. Berkeley, CA 94702
Phone	510 204-0767
Website	www.ohmegasalvage.com
Days & hours of operation	Mon.–Sat. 9 AM–5 PM Sun. 11 AM–5 PM

Description

If you're renovating an older home, or just trying to give your newer home personality, shop here. They sell architectural items salvaged from homes all over the nation. You can buy doors for as little as $100, or spend $3,500 and get a redwood-burl pocket door with Eastlake hardware, made in 1890. The range of items is like that: you'll find windows for just a few bucks, or stained-glass treasures for $1,000 or more. There are two buildings, across the street from each other. The one on the east side features many more bathroom fixtures and some lamps, while on the west side larger items are sold, and there's an indoor gallery of antique and vintage bathroom fixtures.

Omega Lighting Design

Address	2204 San Pablo Avenue Berkeley, CA 94708
Phone	510 843-3636
Website	www.omegatoo.com
Days & hours of operation	Mon.–Sat. 10 AM–6 PM

Description

Down the street from Ohmega Salvage, this store is like the cleaned-up cousin. You can have your vintage and antique lights repaired here, or check out the restored lights for sale on the showroom floor. They also have reproduction lighting spanning from the Victorian era through the 1950s. If you just have an idea for a lamp, they can make it happen. This store also sells reproductions and new designs of antique-looking sinks and bathroom fixtures. None of it is cheap: a small pedestal corner sink can run $700, but when you're restoring a home, your budget has to be flexible. They also sell Mechanical Age pendant lamps, designed and made locally, that would be at home in any loft. They cost about $229.

San Francisco Victoriana

Address	2070 Newcomb Avenue San Francisco, CA 94124
Phone	415 648-0313
Website	www.Sfvictoriana.com
Days & hours of operation	Mon.–Fri. 7:30 AM – 4 PM

Description

Finding this place is not easy. Tucked away next to a freeway underpass, and down an all but dirt road, San Francisco Victoriana is a find in several ways. The company started back in 1972 by building complete Victorian facades and helping restore San Francisco to its original pre-1908 earthquake beauty. Now the folks here sell you the architectural ornaments and let you do the restoration. There are woodwork and plaster pieces for Traditional, Victorian, and Contemporary buildings. Some of the city's most beautiful homes were renovated using items found here. If you need a whole house makeover or just a few pieces, these guys can help. They sell crown molding, wainscoting, banisters, and hand-cast plaster details, and if you need something they don't have, it can be custom made.

The Molding Company

Address	2310 Bates Avenue, Suite D Concord, CA 94520
Phone	925 798-7525
Website	www.themouldingcompany.com
Days & hours of operation	Mon.–Fri. 7 AM–5 PM Sat. 9 AM–2 PM

Description

Also locations in Santa Clara and Millbrae

Located in an industrial park, this store has paint-grade molding, wainscoting, and trim, and it offers those items in oak, maple, alder, and cherry — all in stock and ready for immediate pickup or delivery to a jobsite. This is where many contractors and local suppliers buy their moldings and trim pieces. You can cut out the middleman and save 25% or more by doing your own shopping. The staff is helpful, and they understand that you need guidance, since, unlike them, you don't deal with molding and trim every day.

This and That

Address	1701 Rumrill Blvd. San Pablo, CA 94806
Phone	510 232-1273
Website	www.thisandthatreuse.com
Days & hours of operation	Mon.–Sat, 8 AM–5 PM

Description

This and That buys, sells, and trades factory closeouts, used building materials, and fixtures. You can buy windows, tubs, cabinets, and bathroom fixtures here at prices approaching half off, and sometimes the deals are even better. Old doors are beautiful, but can be hard to deal with since they aren't pre-hung. Not anymore — This and That has a machine that re-hangs salvaged doors with the frame and hardware customers need for easy installation.

Urban Ore

Address	900 Murray Street Berkeley, CA 94710
Phone	510 841-7283
Website	www.urbanore.com
Days & hours of operation	Mon.–Sat. 8:30 AM–7 PM Sun. 10 AM–7 PM

Description

Urban Ore has a mission: "To End the Age of Waste." To that end, they salvage reusable and recyclable items from the dump, and they recycle items brought to their facility. Sinks, bathtubs, windows, and about 3,500 unique doors in over twenty distinct categories are on sale at all times. There's hardware, used furniture, appliances, even records, books, and clothing. The prices are more like Salvation Army than Restoration hardware, so taking up the cause of zero waste also makes you wealthier.

12

Kitchen and Tableware

Biro & Sons Silversmith

Address	1160 Folsom Street San Francisco, California 94103
Phone	415 431-3480 (office)
Website	www.biroandsons.com
Days & hours of operation	Call for hours.

Description

How good are these guys? They worked on The America's Cup! Biro & Sons, Inc. is one of the last small, family-owned silversmith shops offering custom work, repair, and plating. Need a piece replaced or even recreated? They can do it. Walk in and a silversmith greets you — an actual silversmith, who'll discuss your needs with you and eventually come up with the work to be done and a price. Biro & Sons silver plated a belt buckle for me. Back in the 1970s a few Channel 7 belt buckles were made. I coveted one like you wouldn't believe, and finally got my hands on one. Since it was the 1970s, the buckles were made of burnished brass. I rushed to have mine silvered. The cost? $125. The work? Perfect!

Columbus Cutlery

Address	358 Columbus Avenue San Francisco, CA 94133
Phone	415 362-1342
Website	www.northbeachshop.com/pages/ columbuscutlery.htm
Days & hours of operation	Mon. Tues. Thurs. Fri. Sat. 9:30 AM–5 PM

Description

Walking into this store is like traveling back in time — try North Beach, circa 1963. A very small shop, it has room for just a few people behind the counter and a few in front of it. Knives and other sharp objects are everywhere, making the selection here about as good as any you'll find. Prices are better than most cutlery stores. I recently picked up a couple of corkscrews as gifts for $45 dollars, about $5 less than I saw a few blocks away. The service is outstanding: the women behind the counter answer all your questions and will gift-wrap your purchase, too. If you already own quality knives, bring them here for repair and sharpening.

Cutlery Works

Address	Chico Mall Chico, CA 95928
Phone	530 343-0655
Website	No working website found.
Days & hours of operation	Mon.–Sat. 10:0 AM–9 PM Sun. Noon–6 PM

Description

If you ever wanted to put a beautiful girl on a spinning wheel and throw knives at her, this is the store for you. It's a classic mall cutlery shop that doesn't act like one. Here knives are very accessible to the newbie, and the prices are crazy good. Unique to this shop is its subspecialty — throwing knives. I walked in to kill a few minutes while my family was shoe shopping, and I ended up getting a tutorial on knife throwing. How's that for a good afternoon? The physics was explained, and I learned the right way to throw each type of knife. I walked out with a set of throwing knives as a gift for the only person I knew who would appreciate them. He did. I'm not saying you should drive all the way to Chico just for this shop, but if you're tubing the Sacramento River anyway, you might as well drop in. Throwing knives are as low as $20 a set.

East Bay Restaurant Supply

Address	49 Fourth Street Oakland, CA 94607
Phone	510 465-4300
Website	www.eastbayrestaurantsupply.com
Days & hours of operation	Mon.–Sat. 8 AM–5 PM

Description

There's also a store in Sacramento.

Family owned since 1934, East Bay Restaurant Supply is one of the largest supply houses in the restaurant business. Walk in the door and it feels like you've just entered a Costco for cooks. Set up for the professional restaurant chef, the deals are too hard to pass up for weekenders like you and me. Need steak knives? Pick up a dozen here for less than $10, or go for it and get a better set for $16. If you want a restaurant-quality pizza tray, they've got it for $6. A walk-in refrigerator is on sale here for about six grand, but smaller, double-door fridges on wheels that would look great in a loft sell for less than you'd pay for an everyday refrigerator at a home appliance store. Entertain a lot? Pick up an industrial icemaker here for $2025.

Heritage House

Address	2190 Palou Avenue San Francisco, CA 94124
Phone	800 776-6873
Website	www.Heritagehouse.net
Days & hours of operation	Mon.–Fri. 10 AM–6 PM Sat. 11 AM–5 PM

Description

This store is tucked away in a San Francisco industrial district off of Highway 101. It takes a little effort to get there, but the payoff is tremendous. Walk through the front door and the place doesn't look like much, but walk back into the showroom and the sparkle and bling just about knock your eyes out of your sockets: 1,800 patterns from more than a hundred manufacturers are on display. Discounts range from 20% to 50%. The service doesn't stop after you take your items home, either: Heritage House offers a unique guarantee — if a piece you buy here ever breaks, no matter the reason, you can replace it for half price.

Meyer Corporation

Address	One Meyer Plaza Vallejo, CA 94590
Phone	707 551-2800
Website	www.meyer.com
Days & hours of operation	Call for dates, times, and locations.

Description

There's also a store in Fairfield.

Meyer is one the world's largest cookware manufacturers. You might not recognize the company name, but it's responsible for brands like Farberware, KitchenAid, and Circulon. Cookware and tableware bearing the names of Rachael Ray and Paula Deen originate here, too. For the past fifteen years, this Bay Area-based company has opened its warehouses and thrown an annual party that features a big sale, recycling of old cookware, and raffles. Best of all, cookware, bakeware, oven-to-table stoneware, teakettles, kitchen tools, cutlery, pantryware, and other kitchen accessories are discounted between 30% and 70%. There's only one sale each year, and it usually runs from late November to early December.

Replacements

Address	1089 Knox Road Greensboro, NC 27420
Phone	800 737-5223
Website	www.Replacements.com
Days & hours of operation	9 AM–10 PM (ET) every day

Description

Okay, it's not in the Bay Area, but this is the largest collection of tableware on the planet. Really. No one even debates that. Replacements stocks 366,897 patterns in a warehouse filled with fine china, silver, pewter, crystal, and all manner of tableware accessories. They have patterns and pieces dating back to the 1700s. Every day they add thousands of pieces to the collection, so if you really want something, it's bound to end up here eventually. They've become pretty famous, but the renown hasn't ruined them. Customer service is what these guys are all about! Send them the name of your pattern and they'll send you a free price list for all the pieces.

The Wok Shop

Address	718 Grant Avenue San Francisco, CA 94108
Phone	415 989-3797
Website	www.wokshop.com
Days & hours of operation	10 AM–6 PM every day

Description

This place has every imaginable wok and accessory, and the prices are Chinatown good. You can get a traditional cast-iron wok here for under $10. Even with all the many woks here, you have to work pretty hard to spend more than $25. The vibe is fun and welcoming, both for wok pros and those who just want to learn. On "Wok Wednesdays," a group of enthusiasts come to cook their way through Grace Young's cookbook *Stir-Frying to the Sky's Edge.* I can't think of a better way to get started or to up your skill level. All manner of Asian cookware and accessories are offered here and priced well.

13

Fabric, Arts, and Crafts

Britex Fabrics

Address	146 Geary Street San Francisco, CA 94108
Phone	415 392-2910
Website	www.britexfabrics.com
Days & hours of operation	Mon.–Sat. 10 AM–6 PM

Description

Britex Fabrics has been doing business just off of Union Square for sixty Years. It's a San Francisco institution, with four floors of the world's most wonderful fabrics and related supplies. There are occasional sales and a remnant area, but for the most part you come here for the friendly service and the amazing selection. Visit a couple of times and they'll be calling you by name.

East Bay Depot for Creative Reuse

Address	4695 Telegraph Avenue Oakland, CA 94609
Phone	510 547-6470
Website	www.creativereuse.org
Days & hours of operation	11 AM–6 PM daily

Description

Voted "Best Craft Supplies" by nearly every publication, the East Bay Depot is contains 4,500 square feet of reused materials suitable for art, educational projects, and household use. Candles, folders, wires, and yarn are available at remarkably low prices — cheaper still for teachers. This nonprofit was started by two teachers, and they remember their roots.

Fabric Outlet

Address	2109 Mission St. San Francisco, CA 94110
Phone	415 552-4525
Website	www.fabricoutletsf.com
Days & hours of operation	Mon.–Sat. 10 AM–7 PM

Description

This store is located in the middle of the Mission District, so getting here can be trying, but once inside you'll know why you braved the traffic. Discount fabrics — lots of discount fabrics — at prices that will make even non-sewers want to get in on the action. The always-changing selection includes Hello Kitty cloth and pre-quilted material. Discounts range from 20%–40%. To get the best deals, go online before you visit the store. You'll find many specials and discount coupons on the website.

Mendel's

Address	1556 Haight Street San Francisco, CA 94117
Phone	415 621-1287
Website	www.mendels.com
Days & hours of operation	Mon.–Sun. 11 AM–4:50 PM

Description

What if there was an art supply and fabric dealer in the middle of The Haight that had the worldview of its neighborhood? You don't have to ponder that — Mendel's is already here. If you want the best in tie-dye materials, or gauze and supplies to make masks, Mendel's has it. Posters celebrating the Haight-Ashbury neighborhood sell for $9, and fabrics that can only be described as, well, far out (forgive me, please). The great thing about locally owned stores is that they reflect their neighborhoods. Mendel's does more than that — it moves it forward.

Richard's Crafts

Address	225A Alamo Plaza Alamo, CA 94507
Phone	925 820-4731
Website	www.richardsartsandcrafts.com
Days & hours of operation	Mon.–Fri. 9:30 AM–8 PM Sat. 9:30 AM–6 PM Sun. 11 AM–5:30 PM

Description

There's also a Livermore location.

Richard's is one of those neighborhood stores that all the locals knows about but that no one outside of their area has heard of. Well, remember the name. Richard's is a full-service crafts store that offers deep discounts. The best deals come on seasonal merchandise after the season has ended, but even preseason, the deals here beat many of the national chains. Party supplies, scrap booking, and a very impressive supply of candles are available. Framing is a good deal here, too.

SFMOMA Rental Gallery
(San Francisco Museum of Modern Art)

Address	Building A, Ft. Mason Center San Francisco, CA 94123
Phone	415 441-4777
Website	www.sfmoma.org
Days & hours of operation	Tues.–Sat. 11:30 AM–5:30 PM

Description

Walking into this SFMOMA outpost is a treat. A loft space located at Ft. Mason, the Artists Gallery represents Bay Area artists at all stages of their careers. The bargain here is the curated rental gallery. For as little as $25 dollars a month you can take artwork home, hang it on a wall, and live with it long enough to see if you'd like to buy it. You can not only take a test drive but you can work with a staff member to find the right pieces for your environment and tastes, whether at home or at work. A portion of your rental payment will go toward the purchase price. Available art includes paintings, drawings, photos, and sculpture.

14

Toys and Hobbies

Ambassador Toys

Address	186 West Portal Avenue San Francisco, CA. 94127
Phone	415 759-TOYS (8697)
Website	www.ambassadortoys.com
Days & hours of operation	Daily, 10 AM–7 PM

Description

*Other locations in San Francisco,
Palo Alto, and Truckee*

Ambassador Toys carries many of the big sellers and big brands you would expect to find here; however, they specialize in high-end, real wood, and antique reproductions (think tin rocket ships). They pride themselves on their careful selection, including many educational and traditional toys. Since there are so few toy stores left these days, Saturday morning at Ambassador can be a madhouse! I say that in the best possible way. It feels like a celebration as families run in to pick up gifts before heading out to birthday parties. What makes the pre-party stops all the better is the free on-the-spot gift-wrapping. There are occasional sale items, but that's not really what this place is about. It's about getting a great, fast, gift-wrapped gift that you'll be proud to give.

Chan's Trains and Hobbies

Address	2450 Van Ness Avenue San Francisco CA 94109
Phone	415 885-2899
Website	www.chanstrains.com
Days & hours of operation	Mon.–Sat. 10 AM–6 PM Sun. Noon–5 PM

Description

This little store has been open since 1973, but it seems more like a place from the 1950s. It has model trains of every gauge and price point. If you're looking for an inexpensive train set or a Thomas the Tank Engine for your niece or nephew, Chan's has it. But if you're looking for that hard-to-find engine for $1,000, they have that too. Chan's buys, sells, and repairs trains, and all the major names are here: Lionel, American Flyer, Kato, and the rest. Model train enthusiasts build their vacations around visiting this store. Model cars from Revell (there's a name from your childhood) and metal scale models are sold here, too. They also have a nice collection of balsawood and pre-made balsawood airplanes. Pick up one of these for a couple bucks and head down to the Marina Green.

Chinatown Kite Shop

Address	717 Grant Avenue San Francisco, CA 94108
Phone	415 989-5182
Website	www.chinatownkite.com
Days & hours of operation	Call for hours.

Description

Right on Grant Street in the center of Chinatown, this family-owned kite shop has been selling kites at this location for over forty years. They must be doing something right. Walk into the store and all sizes and shapes of kites are hanging from the ceiling and walls, and the clerk is happy to help you find the perfect one. I've seen kites here for as little at $3 and for as much as $50. There are Angry Bird kites, traditional Chinese kites, SpongeBob, and Surfboard kites. Since the owners make many of these kites, you can design and build your own if you're willing to buy in bulk.

Franciscan Hobbies

Address	1920 Ocean Avenue San Francisco, CA 94127
Phone	415 584-3919
Website	www.Franciscanhobbies.com
Days & hours of operation	Tues.–Thurs. and Sat. 10 AM–6 PM Fri. 10 AM–7 PM Sun. Noon–5 PM

Description

You have got to see this place! It looks like a store taken out of a twelve-year-old-boy's dreams. Cars, trains, airplanes and giant ships. Within minutes of walking in, your head is spinning, and you're convinced you need a radio-controlled car... or airplane... or boat... or maybe a train set. I'm not kidding. If you have a kid in your life, plan a Saturday trip here and be ready to spend some quality time with model rockets. They not only stock a huge array of traditional hobby store items, but also offer expert advice to help you move along with your hobby. Buy a starter train set and then expand. Testors paints (remember that name?) and all manner of accessories are sold here, too, along with model cars, train sets, and radio-controlled everything starting at around $50 and going up to several thousand dollars for die-hard fans. There's also a great selection of hobbyist balsawood airplanes starting at under $10.

House of Humor

Address	747 El Camino Real Redwood City, CA 94063
Phone	650 368-5524
Website	www.thehouseofhumor.com
Days & hours of operation	Mon.-Sat. 10 AM–7 PM Sun. 11 AM–5 PM

Description

You can't miss this place, what with the colorful building front that announces it. When I was a kid, House of Humor dealt mainly in fake dog poop and fake plastic ice cubes with flies inside. Now the emphasis has switched to party supplies, wigs, and costumes. Honestly, if there's a costume you want, they must have it here. There are about a thousand, and they range in price from $2 for a set of cat whiskers to a Star Wars Storm Trooper's getup for $1,000. Along with the costumes are hundreds of wigs in every style and color. If there's a wig you want for a night out, it's hard to imagine it wouldn't be in stock. There are some sales, and you can find prices discounted as much as 50% off. They also sell lingerie. Why? I don't know, but I'm certainly not opposed to it.

15

Sport, Skate, and Bicycle

ALITE Designs

Address	2505 Mariposa Street San Francisco, CA 94110
Phone	Tel: 415 626-1526 Fax: 415 651-8899
Website	info@alitedesigns.com www.alitedesigns.com
Days & hours of operation	Fri. Noon–6 PM

Description

Alite Designs is reinventing the outdoor life. Designers here are dedicated to smaller, lighter designs for camping and other outdoor activities. The S.H. (Sexy Hotness) sleeping bag designed here and sold for $149 has legs and feet — you can actually walk around in the thing, and you can zip it together with another bag (thus the name). The Monarch chair, which sells for $63, folds to the size of a parka and weighs about the same. Bring one of these to a soccer game and you'll be the star. Colorful nesting eating utensils sell for $4, and the cardboard put-it-together-yourself birdhouse sells for $5. But here's the real secret of this place: You don't actually have to buy the stuff — they'll lend it to you for free! They have six sets of camping equipment available for borrowing, which include a super-light tent and other gear. Unique dog accessories are also sold here.

Big Dreams

Address	2140 Livingston Street Oakland, CA 94606
Phone	510 842.0505
Website	www.BigDreamsNow.com
Days & hours of operation	See below

Description

Big Dreams is a dealer in action sports clothes and equipment. Several times a year, it pulls together samples from manufacturers like Red, Anon, Nixon, and Habitat, puts them in the middle of a warehouse, and announces a sale via Facebook. The deals are astounding: 40% off retail for current merchandise — no seconds or four-year-old items here. Those in the know line up hours before the sales begin. The emphasis is on snowboarding, so look for snowboards, accessories, and clothes. Major names like Burton are deeply discounted. There's plenty for surfers and skateboarders, too: wetsuits, board shorts, and shoes from companies like Billabong and Volcom. I'll let you in on a secret: You can call the company during normal working hours, and if someone's there you can go to the warehouse and buy right then! If there's no answer, they aren't there, so don't go. But if they do answer, you might show up and find you have the place entirely to yourself.

Cruz Skate Shop

Address	3165 Mission Street, Suite 101 San Francisco, CA 94110
Phone	415 285-8833
Website	www.cruzskateshop.com
Days & hours of operation	Mon.–Sat. Noon–7 PM Sun. Noon–6 PM

Description

Roller derby is back, and Cruz Skate Shop is at the center of this universe. One of the first stores dedicated to the emerging sport, roller-derby folks gather here just to breathe in the atmosphere. A small, clean space on upper Mission, if you want information about the sport come here. If you want a pair of cheap quad skates to get you started, they sell those for as little as $120, helmets for just $10, and body pads for not much more. If you're already committed to the sport, they can hook you up with skates that cost $700 and more. Also for sale, "artistic roller skates," which are used for another growing skate sport that's like figure skating minus the ice. There's a good selection of skateboard decks, trucks, and wheels, too.

Marin Bikes Factory Store

Address	1090 Folsom Street San Francisco, CA 94103
Phone	415 934-8000
Website	www.marinbikes.com
Days & hours of operation	Mon.–Fri. 11 AM–7 PM Sat.–Sun. 10 AM–6 PM

Description

Marin Bikes manufactures a full range of bicycles, and this is where they sell them direct to the public. They make some of the finest rides in the world, including mountain bikes that are essentially motorcycles with pedals rather than engines. They also sell street bikes and racers. The best deals are found on the ugly duckling or forgotten bicycles. For instance, I saw a pink bike there for half price. A pro mountain bike that sells for $6,000 in bike shops goes for $3,500 here — just because it's last year's model. The standard get-around bike that retails for $600 sells for $375 here. The store feels like a real bike shop, not a warehouse, so the shopping experience is a nice one, too. Also, accessories are well priced.

Play It Again Sports

Address	1150 Contra Costa Blvd. Concord, CA 94523
Phone	925 825-3396
Website	www.Playitagainsportspleasanthill.com
Days & hours of operation	Mon. – Fri. 10AM – 7PM Sat. 10AM – 6pm Sun. Noon-5PM

Description

Six locations in the greater Bay Area

This is a chain of sports stores that specializes in selling that treadmill you bought and never used to someone else who'll buy it and never use it. It's a perfect business model for them and for you. Why pay full price for fitness equipment you'll never use? Save yourself some bucks, buy here, and sell it back after a few months. Okay, things aren't actually that bleak, and the deals here are pretty darn good. Gym gear and equipment for all major sports is bought and sold. Want to try out those new kettlebells without going all in? This is your place. Ready to get better golf clubs or lacrosse gear? Drop by and see if they have what you're looking for. There's a wide range of prices, so know what the stuff sells for new before you shop here. There is a Play It Again Store near you.

Racket Supply

Address	10570 S. De Anza Blvd. Cupertino, CA 95014
Phone	408 873-0148
Website	www.RacketSupply.com
Days & hours of operation	Mon.–Fri. 10 AM–7 PM Sat.–Sun. 11 AM–6 PM

Description

Also in Milpitas at 59 Dempsey Rd.
510 962-3358

Just down the street from Apple's world headquarters in Cupertino is a little store designed to get you racket-ready whether your preferred sport is tennis, badminton, or Ping-Pong. They stock tons of rackets, with all the brands you know: Head, Dunlop, Prince, Wilson, and Victor. Rackets you buy are strung onsite for $10 plus the cost of string. Badminton is getting huge in the Bay Area, and this place has the equipment to get you started off right or help improve your game. For such a small space they pack in the badminton and tennis clothing and equipment, including shoes, bags, balls, and shuttlecocks in feather or nylon. If you're tired of paying for stringing, they also sell machines that help you string your own. Some of the best deals here are on the used rackets, which sell for less than half the original cost. Ask for their current price list. This store will price match on any stock item. BTW, I know what you're thinking: It's table tennis, not Ping-Pong, and the sport uses a "blade," not a racket or paddle. Not everyone agrees with that — sheesh!

Re-Cyclery Bike Thrift Shop

Address	610 4th Street San Rafael, CA 94901
Phone	415 458-2986
Website	www.Tripsforkids.com
Days & hours of operation	Tues.–Fri. Noon–6 PM Sat. and Sun. 10 AM–4 PM

Description

Do well by doing good. Talk about a win-win! Want a thousand-dollar bike and only have $250? These guys have you covered! Want an old beater to get around town safely? They have that too, and for under $100. Who are these folks? They're volunteers for a nonprofit organization called Trips for Kids. This place earns about half of the money used to run a program that introduces at-risk kids to bicycling. It's a thrift shop for bikes where you can buy entire bikes or parts and accessories. The prices are set at thrift-store level, so we're talking about less than $100 for bikes that have been safety checked, cleaned, and inspected. Bicycle clothing, usually so overpriced, isn't here. You can pick up a season of lightly — and some not so lightly — worn cycling clothes for a hundred bucks and hit the road/trail looking like you know what you're doing. Those searching for hard-to-find items often hit pay dirt here. There are some new items, and they're priced well, too. If you have a bike you aren't using, donate it to these guys.

Skates On Haight

Address	1818 Haight Street San Francisco, CA 94117
Phone	415 752-8375
Website	www.skatesonhaight.com
Days & hours of operation	10 AM–6 PM every day

Description

This store is so famous you expect to walk into a warehouse, but what you find is a refined and friendly space that's about the size of your average skate shop. Nonetheless, skaters from around the country show up here just to see the place. The seasoned staff welcomes everyone. Pick out a deck, trucks, and wheels and their techs will put them together and have you rolling out the door in no time. They have a couple of demo boards, so you can skate before you buy. Do it! It's worth the ride just so you can say you've skateboarded in The Haight (no one in San Francisco calls this neighborhood Haight-Ashbury — it's just "The Haight"). They offer a great deal on retro boards. If you remember those small plastic boards from the 1980s, you'll be happy to know they have a bunch on hand in a variety of bright colors. For $54 you can skate the city and still hop on Muni without hitting people with your long board.

Sling It! Lacrosse

Address	Alamo Plaza Suite, 180-A Alamo, CA 94507
Phone	925 820-5802
Website	www.Slingitlacross.com
Days & hours of operation	Mon.–Fri. 10 AM–7 PM Sat.–Sun. 10 AM–5 PM

Description

Other Bay Area locations: San Rafael, Belmont, Redwood City, and San Jose.

This is your one-stop shop for all things lacrosse. The store is packed with everything from coaching gear, training equipment, and clothing, including a large selection of athletic footwear. The friendly and helpful staff will help you wade through the different sizing for your future lacrosse star, and can either help you with individual equipment needs or outfit an entire team. They'll also assemble and string custom sticks for you, based on the athlete's size and level of ability. Look for seasonal markdowns on shorts and practice T-shirts, with some shirts as low as $8. Buy ahead or after season to find name-brand gloves like Brine, Reebok, Nike, and Warrior from 10%–40% off. This is also a good place to go if you're interested in lacrosse-related summer camps and clinics. If you love the sport, you'll love this store.

Soccer Pro

Address	6635 Dublin Blvd. Suite F Dublin, CA 94568
Phone	925 803-4435
Website	www.soccerpro.com
Days & hours of operation	Mon.–Fri. 10 AM–7 PM Sat. 10 AM–5 PM Sun. 11 AM–4 PM

Description

Other Bay Area locations in Pleasant Hill, San Jose, and Redwood City, and in Sacramento

Whether you're a soccer coach, player, or fan, this is your dream store. It has everything imaginable relating to the sport. They've got an entire section of training and coaching gear, jerseys like the pros wear, and all the equipment and clothing you could possibly need to suit up in style. Look for the huge bin of soccer balls in all sizes and colors, and the "wall of socks." They're prepared with everything, no matter what your team colors. You can find racks of Tee shirts, including brands like Nike and Adidas, for $10 each. Look for seasonal shoe sales at up to 20% off, and scrimmage vests in all sizes and colors for $6 each.

Sports Basement

Address	1590 Bryant Street San Francisco, CA 94103
Phone	415 575-3000
Website	www.sportsbasement.com
Days & hours of operation	Mon.–Fri. 9 AM–9 PM Sat.–Sun. 8 AM–8 PM

Description

Also locations in San Francisco's Presidio, Sunnyvale, and Walnut Creek.

This is a fun space for a sporting-goods store: it's a brick warehouse building in a upcoming area of the city. The store is big and offers a huge selection, but it still keeps the feel of a smaller neighborhood store. The company says they pull that off by hiring local coaches and enthusiasts who know the area and the people who shop in the stores. The fixtures here are all handmade locally, and the vibe is pure San Francisco. Part of a small Bay Area-based chain of four stores, Sports Basement is building its reputation by spotlighting local companies and offering free in-store events and great prices. They buy samples from sales reps, and closeout items from manufacturers that produced too many or are trying to offload last year's stuff. There are some excellent prices on running shoes, especially, for some reason, women's running shoes.

Steele's Discount Scuba

Address	5987 Telegraph Avenue Oakland, CA 94609
Phone	510 655-4344
Website	No working website found.
Days & hours of operation	Tues. 4 PM–6 PM Wed. and Fri. 10 AM–6 PM Thurs: 10:30 AM–7 PM Sat. 10 AM–3 PM

Description

I first visited Steele's when I was sixteen years old — pre-Internet (I know, I know). It was renowned for selling scuba gear at the lowest prices in the nation. Since my funds were limited, it drew me like a magnet, and it still draws those looking for deals. The place was dark and scary to me then, and it remains a unique experience today. From the street, Steele's Discount Scuba looks abandoned. Walk in, and you see equipment piled up seemingly without regard to new, used, for sale, or for rent. It's still dark inside, but there's a method to the madness. You go up to the sales counter and find owner Jim Steele and his customers deep in scuba conversation. They welcome you into the club. The equipment prices here are still astounding. Steele has known the makers and importers for decades. He works hard to get you the right gear, and there's never an up-sale. They train divers in nearby pools, and take great pride in their certification process.

The Anchor Shack

Address	5775 Pacheco Blvd. Pacheco, CA 94553
Phone	925 825-4960
Website	www.anchorshack.com
Days & hours of operation	Mon.–Sat. 10 AM–5 PM

Description

You might not think Pacheco would be on the cutting edge of diver education, but then you find The Anchor Shack. The store, which is below street level, looks odd when you drive by, but walk through the front door and you'll find a clean, well-equipped shop that can fulfill all your diving needs. Those looking for scuba certification will find a mellow staff and welcoming vibe. The dive masters are knowledgeable, patient, and all PADI (Professional Association of Diving Instructors) trained. A custom-built — and warm — pool designed specifically for scuba training helps make learning here an exceptional experience. If you train here, you can use the pool and diving equipment at no extra charge for practice during and after your certification training. The Anchor Shack offers diver certification to the highest levels, as well as trips to exotic diving locations. Their rental gear is in excellent shape. This is truly a gathering spot for divers.

Treadmill Outlet

Address	1401 El Camino Real Redwood City, CA 94063
Phone	877 925 5760
Website	www.TreadmillOutlet.com
Days & hours of operation	Mon.–Fri. 11 AM–7 PM Sat.–Sun. 11 AM–5 PM

Description

Before you buy home or professional equipment, come here. This place is packed with treadmills, elliptical trainers, spinners, and recumbent cycles from all the major makers. They promise prices below anywhere else in the country, and to my eye they pull that off every day. To find the best deals ask about their close-out specials, where you'll get as much as 60% off on the biggest names, HealthRider and Nordic track, for example. If you want to rent a piece of machinery, they can do that. Want your treadmill or other equipment repaired? They have parts and trained technicians. They'll even move your treadmill from one location to another or set it up on their showroom floor and sell it on commission. Prices range from as low as $200 for a lightly used treadmill to as much as $4,500, with lots of price points in between. Every type of gym equipment is sold here, including rowers, free weights, and steppers.

16

Music

Amoeba Music

Address	1855 Haight Street San Francisco, CA 94117
Phone	415 831-1200
Website	www.Amoeba.com
Days & hours of operation	Mon.-Sat. 10:30 AM–10 PM Sun. 11 AM — 9 PM

Description

There are also Berkeley and Hollywood locations.

Amoeba Music is located in an abandoned bowling alley near the end of Haight Street, close to Golden Gate Park's Hippie Hill. Amoeba is the landmark now. It has the world's largest selection of LPs, and it carries the largest inventory of previously watched films in the country, on DVD, VHS, Laserdisc, Blu-Ray, PSP, and HD-DVD. Here you can buy, sell, and trade your music, posters, and movies. As you walk through the front door there's a bag check to the left and a buy desk to the right. The desk is staffed with buyers who can make quick decisions on what your merchandise is worth. They'll give you cash or store credit, the credit being worth 30% more. Farther into the store, on the left is the 45 rpm record section, and on the right, collectible rock posters and boxed sets. Walk down a ramp and into the main store and you're surrounded by vinyl and CDs. Every type of music is available, and if what you want isn't here, it soon will be. The best part of this store is the thrill of the hunt, finding that impossible-to-find item.

Dave's Record Shop

Address	2634 San Pablo Avenue Berkeley, CA 94702
Phone	510 666-0336
Website	www.davesrecordshop.com
Days & hours of operation	Tues. – Sat. Noon – 7PM

Description

This is a small store with a big reputation. Dave's Record Shop is a high-end vinyl-only specialty shop. If you're looking to buy or sell perfect or near perfect discs and covers this is your store. Dave Kloski looks to buy and sell only records in pristine condition, so serious collectors don't have to paw through them wondering if they're too scratched to play. Records tend to be in the $10–$20 range, but can go much higher for mint condition hard-to-find items. Recently, a sealed Taj Mahal album — the one with Taj sitting in front of an abandoned house — was on sale for $75. A Guns N' Roses *Appetite for Destruction* was going for $100. If you have a large collection, Dave will come to your house, saving you the drudgery of boxing your albums and dragging them across the Bay Area. Dave promises to pay the highest prices for your records. Put him to the test.

Rasputin Music

Address	2403 Telegraph Avenue Berkeley, CA 94704
Phone	510 848-9004
Website	www.rasputinmusic.com
Days & hours of operation	Mon.–Fri. 11 AM–8 PM Sat 10:30 AM–9 PM Sun. 11:30 AM–8 PM

Description

Six other Bay Area locations, plus Vallejo and Stockton.

I love this small chain's catchphrase: "Rasputin Music and DVDs. Keep'n the Bay Area Bump'n Since 1971." That would be the year before Tower of Power released *Bump City,* a great piece of vinyl you can find here. The albums — CDs and vinyl — come priced from as low as $5, and there's a huge selection in that price range. Unlike many used-record stores, Rasputin carries a selection of comedy albums. Buy Bill Cosby's *Why is there Air?* for $4. Now, there's a night of cheap entertainment for you and your friends. Of course Rasputin buys, sells, and trades, so bring in your old stuff and swap it for something you'll actually watch or listen to. Rasputin hosts quite a few performances, so it's worth keeping track of their calendar. Specials pop up from time to time. If you want high-end items, let them know what you're looking for.

Record Man

Address	1322 El Camino Real Redwood City, CA 94063
Phone	650 368-9065
Website	www.Recordman.com
Days & hours of operation	Mon.–Fri. 10 AM–9 PM Sat. 10 AM–7 PM Sun. 10 AM–6 PM

Description

The Recordman? Oh, yeah, the Recordman! This is one of the premier record stores in the United States. Why? The inventory of records is huge — over a million titles. Floor-to-ceiling shelves are stocked with an impressive collection. In fact, this isn't just a store, it's a complex of three interacting stores: The Record Man, Planet Mix, and The RecordMan Annex. There are huge sections set aside for The Beatles, The Rolling Stones, and Elvis. My favorite Elvis album here is a boxed set of songs picked by fans in Japan. It sells for $20. Pack a lunch — the Recordman will keep you busy all day. The building out back is where the $5 stock is kept, along with video games. DJs love this place because it offers thousands of 45s and 12-inch singles. There are also books on music, and thousands of pieces of sheet music. The annex's inventory consists of posters, magazines, photographs, and music videos. And talk about going old school, check this: a twelve-foot-high wall packed with vintage prerecorded reel-to-reel tapes.

Rooky Ricardo's Records

Address	448 Haight Street San Francisco, CA 94117
Phone	415 864-7526
Website	www.rookyricardos.com
Days & hours of operation	Mon.–Fri. Noon–6 PM Sat.–Sun. Noon–6ish

Description

This is a neighborhood record store in all the best ways. First, the name alone makes it worth checking out. Then there's the time spent in the business: this store has earned the title "institution" by being here, being good, and being inexpensive for twenty-five years. Inside there are plenty of listening stations and thousands of titles. Rooky Ricardo's boasts a stock of over 100,000 45s and 10,000 LPs. There are records from all genres, but the store specializes in Soul, Girl Groups, and Oldies from the 1950s, '60s, and '70s. There are, of course, collectors' items that cost more, but the basic prices are amazing. Standard 45s sell for $2 each or three for $5. LPs generally go for $5–$10. The store is well laid out, making it easy to run in during lunch hour to see if that special record you're looking for is here, and the service is friendly without being overbearing.

17

Gifts

Australian Products Company

Address	3680 Stevens Creek Blvd. San Jose, CA 95117
Phone	408 748-9999
Website	www.aussieproducts.com
Days & hours of operation	Mon.–Fri. 11 AM–7 PM Sat. 11 AM–5 PM Sun. Noon–4 PM

Description

Let's say you're in the market for a didgeridoo. Where would you go? San Jose might not leap to mind, but to an area that prides itself on diversity, the Australian Products Store is a fun addition. In an orange building across the street from the Guitar Center and Frontier Ford, it's packed with all things Australia, including didgeridoos (and videos on how to play them), boomerangs, and all kinds of souvenirs: flags, T-shirts, stuffed Koalas, and outback-style hats and clothing sure to bring out the Crocodile Dundee in you. They also have a couple of aisles of groceries you'd normally find only in the Land Down Under, like Aussie crackers, cookies, teas, plus various health and beauty products. A small frozen food section features items like steak-and-kidney pies and British bangers. There's also a section of sheepskin boots and slippers for sale or order. No Uggs here, but boots and shoes priced at a more reasonable $69–$89 a pair. They can special-order any size they don't have in stock, which can then be shipped to the store for pickup or directly to your home. G'day, mate!

British American Imports

Address	726 - 15th Street San Francisco, CA 94103
Phone	415 863-3300
Website	www.britshoppe.com
Days & hours of operation	Tues.–Sat. 10 AM–5 PM

Description

Okay, all you British expats, we know what you're up to. I first found this little store a few years back, and loved the casual nature of its owner and just how British the store could be. Now there's a huge online presence, too. All the British food you could want is here, including Cadbury Dairy Milk Chocolate, the original Mars Bar, creamed rice, and proper salad cream. They also stock British drugstore items like Cussons Imperial Leather soap. Teas, oh yes, they have teas. The best deals are called "bargain basement," and include china plates, usually $14, selling for $4. If they're part of your china set, or you want them to be, you've struck gold!

Gamago

Address	335 8th Street San Francisco, CA 94103
Phone	415 626-0213
Website	www.Gama-Go.com
Days & hours of operation	Mon.–Fri. Noon–6 PM

Description

"Clever, practical, and original" is the motto here, and Gamago pulls it off. This San Francisco company designs and makes all its own goods. They offer kitchen gadgets, barware, and gifts. A unicorn-inspired corkscrew called the Screwnicorn, and the accordion file that looks like an accordion, go for $10. They also sell the best temporary tattoos I've ever seen, including one pack that resembles letters cut from a magazine, so your temp tat will look like a crazed criminal wrote the message. The price is $6. You know those family stickers you see on the back of minivans, often stick figures? Gamago sells its version of Zombie Family Car Stickers for $8. T-shirts with interesting graphics in men and women's sizes sell for $28, kids' sizes $20. So what's the connection among all these items? Good, interesting, and hip design. To get the best deals, show up for Happy Hour, between noon and 2:00 PM, when everything is discounted 15%.

Irish Castle Gift Shop

Address	537 Geary Street San Francisco, CA 94102
Phone	415 474-7432
Website	No working website found.
Days & hours of operation	Mon.–Sat. 10 AM–6 PM Sun. 10 AM–4 PM

Description

An unexpected find in The Tenderloin, this small store-front is easy to pass by. With just a tiny sign and no Internet presence, it thrives because it is authentic. This high-end Irish gift shop has been here for years, and its clientele is loyal. Dating back to a time when it seemed every other person in San Francisco was Irish, the store was a bit of the Emerald Isle transplanted here, and it still is. Wool sweaters are big sellers since the weather here and in Ireland have a lot in common. Hats, Tees, and Christmas items are big here, too.

Mixcoatl Arts and Crafts

Address	3201 24th Street San Francisco, CA 94110
Phone	415 341-4191
Website	No working website found.
Days & hours of operation	Mon.–Sat. 10 AM–7 PM Sun. 11 AM–6 PM

Description

You can't miss this place. On the corner of 24th and South Van Ness, the entire front of the shop is covered with Mexican wrestling masks. They're fitted to balloons so you can actually see what they would look like on a severed head. If you're planning to get into Mexican wrestling, come by here first. The masks displayed outside sell for $25. Inside, better ones go for $35. Kids' masks are just $12, and if you want a mask attached to a cape, a la Spiderman, you'll spend $18 for the child size. Aside from the wrestling masks, there's fine silver, with earrings starting at just $15. Those colorful carved animals start at $20. The staff is helpful and fun, and without asking will keep you up-to-date on events in the neighborhood.

Piñata Art Studio

Address	4268 Mission Street San Francisco CA 94112
Phone	415 333-8001
Website	www.pinataart.net
Days & hours of operation	Mon.–Fri. 11 AM–6 PM Sat. 10 AM–4 PM

Description

Piñata Art studio offers a huge range of piñatas. The prices range from \$10 for a small figurine to as much as \$75 for a large full-bodied character piñata. Piñatas shaped like soccer balls and Angry Birds sell for \$45. A SpongeBob or Spiderman will cost you \$75. The piñatas are between two and five feet tall. The smaller, rounder objects have just one chamber to fill with candy. Other designs, like dragons, have three chambers. There are dozens of readymade piñatas to pick from, but here's the really cool part: the artist, Romero G. Osorio, will create a custom-made piñata for your event. Give a week's notice, and for \$45–\$75 you'll get a one-of-a-kind work of art.

Rick's Picks

Address	375 Hartz Avenue Danville, CA 94526
Phone	925 837-3325
Website	www.rickspicks.biz
Days & hours of operation	Sun.–Wed. 10 AM–6 PM Thurs.–Sat. 10 AM–8:30 PM

Description

There's a store in Pleasanton, too.

Rick's Picks deals mainly in home accessories and gifts, but there's a lot more going on. The majority of the items come here as samples from tradeshows, but Rick's also cuts special deals with local merchants, suppliers, and businesspeople. On a recent trip to Rick's, I found candy bars for 50 cents, wine for $6, and a folding Beer Pong table for $149. Items come into and leave the store all the time, so it's best to wander through on a regular basis. There are always good deals on toys and wrapping paper, as well as flower-arrangement supplies.

18

Souvenir Stores

Cable Car Museum

Address	1201 Mason Street San Francisco, CA 94108
Phone	415 474-1887
Website	www.cablecarmuseum.org
Days & hours of operation	Open daily except New Year's Day, Easter Sunday, Thanksgiving, and Christmas. April 1–Sept. 30, 10 AM–6 PM Oct. 1–March 31, 10 AM–5 PM

Description

Located in the historic Washington/Mason cable-car barn and powerhouse, the museum and store overlooks the huge engines and winding wheels that pull the cables. Come here for the history. This is a free museum, but it's also a great place to buy a piece of San Francisco. Aside from the graphic Tees, hats, and ornaments, there are items you can buy only here, such as 5½-inch lengths of authentic cable-car cable — taken up during the 1982 rehabilitation program — that sell for $13.99. Or you can pick up a real twenty-pound brass bell, exactly what's used on San Francisco's historic cable cars. The $599 cost is steep, but history and tradition don't come cheap. Art, toys, and models are also for sale; most, but not all, are cable car-related.

Crissy Field Warming Hut and Bookstore

Address	Crissy Field The Presidio San Francisco, CA 94129
Phone	415 561-3040
Website	www.parksconservancy.org/store
Days & hours of operation	Mon.–Fri. 9 AM–5 PM Sat.–Sun. 9 AM–7 PM

Description

This is one of my favorite spots in the city: views of the bridge to die for, fishermen outside on the dock, cyclists pedaling by, and hot coffee. Making the place even better is shopping that helps the local national parks and items you won't be embarrassed about once you get home. There is a revolving collection of crafts from local artisans, posters and prints from local artists, and books by local authors, too. This is a great place to shop for the kids in your life. A message-in-a-bottle kit sells for $10, and T-shirts and games for kids of all ages are available.

Golden Gate Bridge Gift Shop

Address	Golden Gate Bridge Toll Plaza San Francisco, CA
Phone	415 923-2333
Website	www.goldengatebridge.org
Days & hours of operation	9 AM–6 PM daily

Description

The Golden Gate Bridge is an iconic image of San Francisco, so why not own it? Here at the gift shop, which helps support Golden Gate National Park, there are amazing one-of-a-kind posters and photographs starting at $10. T-shirts commemorating the bridge's 75th anniversary sell for $18, kids sizes $14. A way-cool biking shirt goes for $75. One brand-new item is the Golden Gate Bridge cable pen, produced with an International Orange cable casing that sells for $28. There are always a few items on sale, but the best way to get a deal is to join Golden Gate National Parks Conservancy for $35. You help preserve the natural beauty of the area, and the membership gets you 15% off anything you buy at the gift shop.

Oakland Museum of California

Address	1000 Oak Street Oakland, CA 94607
Phone	510 318-8400
Website	www.museumca.org
Days & hours of operation	Wed.–Sun. 11 AM–5 PM

Description

This place concentrates on what makes California special, showcasing the Golden State in arts, craft, history, and nature. Along with hats, Tees, and bookmarks, you'll find a unique collection of items curated like a gallery show. There are kids' books like *Mother Goose in California,* which goes for $17, and a Michael Wertz silkscreen print sells for $25. Guides and hiking maps are $8.50. You don't have to pay for museum entry to enter the store, which makes this a nice shopping stop during gift-buying season.

San Francisco Railway Museum and Gift Shop

Address	77 Steuart Street San Francisco, CA 94105
Phone	415 974-1948
Website	www.streetcar.org
Days & hours of operation	Tues.–Sun. 10 AM–6 PM

Description

Though it sits at one of the most beautiful corners in the city, the SF Railway Museum & Gift Shop is easy to miss. The museum, across the street from the historic Ferry Building, tells the story of the time-honored streetcars that run through San Francisco alongside the cable cars. San Francisco is one of the few remaining places in the world where you can ride vintage streetcars in, as the museum says, their "natural habitat." The gift shop has some of the most beautiful posters anywhere in the city. They all feature the streetcars and all have a vintage feel. Books sold here tell the story of the streetcars and the story of San Francisco, an urban space that truly was built by public transportation. T-shirts sell for $17, posters $18, and small kitchen magnets with the same image are just $5.

19

Computers

Bay Area Computer Man

Address	3680 Stevens Creek Blvd. Suite F San Jose, CA 95117
Phone	408 249-4821
Website	www.bayareacomputerman.com
Days & hours of operation	Mon.–Fri. 9 AM–7 PM Sat. 9 AM–6 PM Sun. 10 AM–6 PM

Description

Back in the day, there used to be small, friendly independent computer shops all over the Bay Area. There are still a number out there, and Bay Area Computer Man is among the best. Here a friendly and knowledgeable staff will repair your computer — if possible — right on the spot. They also sell parts, offer advice, and sell used computers cheap. How about a Mac G4 for $49, or an IBM with a 40GB hard drive for $99? On a recent visit, I found a Toshiba laptop selling for $175. No, it wasn't state of the art, but perfectly good for writing up a work report or term paper. They also make house/business calls.

Berkeley Typewriter and Clark Business Machine

Address	1823 University Avenue Berkeley, CA 94703
Phone	510 843-2326
Website	No working website found.
Days & hours of operation	Mon.–Fri. 9 AM–6 PM Sat. 10 AM–6 PM

Description

Berkeley Typewriter is on University Avenue, where it's been for the past eighty years, just a few blocks from campus. What might at first seem like a dying business is actually enjoying a renaissance. Typewriter sales are booming. A few customers are looking for a new electric model to type addresses on envelopes and the like, but most of the new customers are in their twenties and thirties and like the look and feel of the old business machines. Here the manager pirates parts from other old typewriters and makes the machines work like new. You can buy a typewriter here for as little as $150 or as much as a thousand. If you have an old IBM Selectric you want brought back to life, they can handle that. Many of the typewriters here have been painted red — it seems young people like red typewriters.

Renew Computers

Address	446 DuBois Street San Rafael, CA 94901
Phone	415 457-8801
Website	www.renewcomputers.com
Days & hours of operation	Mon.–Fri. 9 AM–5 PM Sat. 10 AM–3 PM

Description

Need a computer? How about one for $219? If you're not one of those folks who've just got to have the latest and greatest, you can save a lot of money buying a computer that was just discarded by someone who is. This store serves two main purposes: First, they'll safely dispose of your old computers, TVs, and other electronics. Then, computers worth recycling are repaired, refurbished, and put up for sale. They offer 90-day warranties and in-home setup, and training is available if you need it. The store is tucked away in an industrial area of San Rafael, a couple of blocks behind the Best Buy and across from Jackson's Hardware. They accept all electronics for disposal or recycling at no charge, but don't expect a tax refund — this is a for-profit business. You do get brownie points, though, for being green.

WeirdStuff Warehouse

Address	384 West Caribbean Drive Sunnyvale, CA 94089
Phone	408 743-5650
Website	www.weirdstuff.com
Days & hours of operation	Mon.–Sat. 9:30 AM–6 PM Sun. 11 AM–5 PM

Description

This old-age home for technology could only be found in Silicon Valley. Buried in an industrial park, Weird-Stuff Warehouse has been around for twenty years. Whether you're a high-tech techie or collect relics of the high-tech past, this is a must-see — 10,000 sq. ft. space stacked high with rows and rows of computers, electronics, hardware, software, cables, books, and office equipment. Parts end up here from last year's models and last decade's failures. Collectors paw through this stuff like prospectors looking for gold. Remember Sun Microsystems? Parts are available here. Keyboards sell for a buck, working computers for $50. Working monitors start at $10. You could easily piece together a simple computer for under $80. Laptops start at $135. Along with the computers, you'll find ancient laser discs for $8, WALK / DON'T WALK signs for $20, and heavy-duty shipping containers for $45.

20

Photo Supplies and Electronics

Adolph Gasser

Address	181 Second Street San Francisco, CA 94105
Phone	415 495-3852
Website	www.gassersphoto.com
Days & hours of operation	Mon.–Fri. 9 AM–6 PM Sat. 10 AM–5 PM

Description

This has been the go-to photography store for many of the city's professional photographers for decades. The store offers sales, service, and rentals. If you need it, these guys have it, and at a good price. There are new and used cameras and a repair facility, and the film lab is still up and running. Color and black-and-white film processing begins at $4 for developing and 25 cents per print. Super 8 movie-film processing, B/W or color, is just $25. If you want to do it yourself, they sell darkroom chemicals and equipment. There's a big video department as well, and the staff offers expert advice. There's a rental department for professionals, but it works for you, too, since you can try out the gear before you buy. For the best deal on rentals, show up on Wednesday or Friday between 3:00 and 5:45 when walk-ins get 40% off. If you're a photographer/filmmaker on a budget, this is how you get the job done. Classes and workshops start at $159, for students $139. Passport photos cost $10, and will probably be the best shot of you ever taken.

Glass Key Photo

Address	442 Haight Street San Francisco, CA 94117
Phone	415 829-9946
Website	www.GlassKeyPhoto.com
Days & hours of operation	Mon.–Sun. Noon–6 PM

Description

Kodak files for bankruptcy, longtime photography shops have stopped selling film cameras, consumers are digitizing their old slides — sounds like a great time to open a camera store devoted to film. So Matt Osborn got Glass Key Photo up and going. He says the store carries more brands of film than anyplace in San Francisco, and my spot check proved that correct. Kodak, Fuji, Rollei, Efke, Adox and more are here. They have chemicals for developing, paper, and ink. There's a fun display of film cameras, which are for sale, including the small ones they used to give away at carnivals for knocking down the milk bottles. The big seller here is new film for a very old camera: the Polaroid Land Camera has become a top seller to young hipsters and artists, but finding the instant-picture film is near impossible. They have it here. And root beer. Matt likes root beer, so he sells that, too.

Ham Radio Outlet

Address	510 Lawrence Expressway, #102 Sunnyvale, CA 94085
Phone	408 736-9496
Website	www.hamradio.com
Days & hours of operation	Mon–Sat. 10 AM–5:30 PM

Description

Who knew that ham radio operators had a vibrant community? The Internet and cell phones may have taken over our lives, but they haven't replaced ham radios and their operators, who are still out there staying in touch and performing important community services — especially during natural disasters and other calamities. The Ham Radio Outlet is a family-owned business with twelve stores nationwide, including this one in Sunnyvale and one in Oakland. Ham Radio Outlet touts itself as the largest ham radio dealership in the world. I haven't been to every store, but I don't doubt them. This store is jammed with the newest, best, and more affordable used ham equipment. A good way to get started is to buy pre-owned equipment. The personnel here are experts, and are ham operators themselves. For the best deals, look for online specials and coupons. If you'd like to learn more about the world of ham radio, you can do it here. They'll hook you up with all the study materials you need, along with lists of times and locations for licensing exams.

International Spy Shop

Address	555 Beach St. San Francisco, CA 94133
Phone	415 775-4779
Website	www.internationalspyshop.com
Days & hours of operation	Mon.–Sun. 11 AM–8 PM Open daily in summer, 10 AM–10 PM

Description

The name of this store is the International Spy Shop. Do I really have to say anything more to get you interested? If you want to spy or hide from spies, these guys can help you. The store is lined with shelves displaying the most amazing products. There are safes hidden in hollowed-out books and wall outlets. There are nanny cams hidden in clocks and Teddy bears. For $15 you can get "TV Terror," a palm-sized device that intercepts and clones a TV's remote-control coding information, putting you always in charge of the TV set, even if it's not yours. Anti-bugging devices and services are offered, and so are GPS tracking devices. Prices range from a couple hundred dollars to a few thousand. The shop offers a price match, too, so do your homework before you buy. Warning: If you hang out here long enough, you'll think you're being spied on or you'll want to spy on someone else.

San Jose Camera and Video

Address	1600 S. Winchester Blvd. Campbell, CA 95008
Phone	408 374-1880
Website	www.Sanjosecamera.com
Days & hours of operation	Mon.–Wed. Fri.–Sat. 10 AM–6 PM Thurs. 10 AM–8 PM Sun. Noon–5 PM

Description

This is your daddy's camera store, just updated with digital gear and video. San Jose Camera and Video, which is actually in Campbell, has been in business since 1929, offering a large selection of name-brand camera equipment and accessories for less. The brick building it's in seems huge on the outside, but it's not so intimidating once you walk in and are greeted by the friendly and helpful staff. They carry all the major brands you'd expect: Canon, Nikon, Olympus, and Sony. They try hard to compete with Internet pricing — no easy task for a photography store. The best way to search out deals here is to go online first and check out their specials and rebates. Recent bargains included the popular Canon EOS Rebel (models T3i & T2i) matched with lenses, at savings of up to $300. Inexpensive digital photography and lighting classes are offered for about $75. They also do repairs, and there's a great selection of camera bags and carrying cases.

World of Stereo

Address	1080 Market Street San Francisco, CA 94102
Phone	Tel: 415 626-6554 Fax: 415 626-9710
Website	www.WorldOfStereo.com
Days & hours of operation	Mon. – Sat. 10AM – 7:30PM Sun. 10AM – 6PM

Description

Also in Petaluma

This store is in a rough-looking part of town, but it's worth the trip. You'll find DJ equipment stacked floor to ceiling. If you're just starting out mixing, and are looking for a controller for a couple hundred bucks, they've got you covered. If you're a big-name DJ looking for gear, they also offer the best and most expensive. New or used, they can take care of folks who are into old-school scratching and those who want the latest in digital DJing. Marvin, the owner, keeps the prices as low as the Internet wholesalers' — sometimes better. One example of a great price is the Numark NS6 controller/mixer, seen around town for $1,300. It sells here for $999. Every imaginable accessory is available, along with recording equipment, lighting, microphones, and software, all at reduced prices. They even offer free shipping anywhere in the lower forty-eight states — with no minimum purchase! There's been a music store in this location since the bank that started here went out of business during the Great Depression, which just goes to show that good music outlasts money.

Video Only

Address	655 Du Bois Street San Rafael, CA 94901
Phone	415 547-4518
Website	www.Videoonly.com
Days & hours of operation	Mon.–Fri. 10 AM–9 PM Sat. 10 AM–7 PM Sun. 11 AM–6 PM

Description

Five store locations throughout the Bay Area

This is an old school chain offering huge discounts. The company says it tells customer, "Don't be sorry ... shop around," because they know the prices offered here are low. In fact they're often the lowest available; still, take their advice and shop around. All the major brands are here: Sony, JVC, Toshiba, and the rest. The experience of buying here is like TV shopping in the old days: you and a real-live salesperson talking to each other. The company so believes in this process that it refuses to sell on the Internet. The salespeople will take the time to educate you, so ask questions and take your time.

21

Pet Stores

6th Avenue Aquarium

Address	425 Clement Street San Francisco, CA 94118
Phone	415 668-7190
Website	www.6thaveaqurium.com
Days & hours of operation	Mon.–Fri. 11 AM–10 PM Sat.–Sun. 10 AM–10 PM

Description

Regardless of the posted official hours, I don't think I've ever seen this place closed. Any time of day or night it's like walking into another world: it's dark, there are black lights, and the smell of fish is in the air. 6th Avenue Aquarium has a huge variety of fish and some of the best prices ever seen for plants, tanks, and fish. Every Sunday there's a special "I love Sundays" wholesale-to-the-public event. It starts at exactly 10:00 AM and the best items go fast. The sale features marine fish and coral. Sample prices: damsels $1; turbo snails $1; Percula clownfish $3. There's also a big assortment of tanks, aquariums, and even garden ponds.

Alamo Hay & Grain

Address	3196 Danville Blvd. Alamo, CA 94507
Phone	925 837-4994
Website	No working website found.
Days & hours of operation	Mon.–Sat. 8 AM–6 PM Sun. 9 AM–4 PM

Description

This might be the only drive-through pet store in the country. You can drive right into the middle of the retail space, load up your fifty-pound bag of dog food, hay for the horses, and other items, and then head on out. Many pet stores say they're convenient, but these guys prove it every day. Alamo, with its large lots and agricultural past, has many pets not found in most suburbs, including horses, chickens, ducks, and bunnies, the smaller of which they sell here. There's also food for all of them. This is not your cuddly pet store; the people are nice, well informed, and assume that you are going to eat some of these animals — or at least put them to work. This place is little changed since it open back in 1962, and that's a good thing. Here, the farm smells of hay and alfalfa mingle with the aroma of dog food.

Bogie's Discount Pet Food & Supplies

Address	37085 Post Street Fremont, CA 94536
Phone	510 795-6000
Website	www.bogiespet.com
Days & hours of operation	Mon. Wed. Thurs.–Fri. 10 AM–8 PM Tues. 10 AM–9 PM Sat. 8:30 AM–7 PM Sun. 10 AM–6 PM

Description

The first time you come here it can be hard to find the front door, which is out back, but once inside you'll find a huge selection, with great prices on bulk feed for household animals, livestock, and horses. A unique part of this operation is the time they take to make sure your pets get the perfect food for their diet. They are *way* serious about this, and if you're looking for a vegan or gluten-free diet for your dog, they can get it done. This is a full-service pet center with grooming, vaccines, and classes. Puppy training classes are held every Wednesday night, and walk-ins are welcome — just pay $8. All the usual pet supplies are here, along with a small but sturdy selection of fish. Dog food is heavy, and in many pet stores you'll see customers struggle to drag those big bags out the door. Not here. They get the bags for you. Among the best deals are the specials on bulk food and pet care.

Catnip & Bones

Address	2220 Chestnut Street San Francisco, CA 94123 Neighborhood: Marina/Cow Hollow
Phone	415 359-9100
Website	No working website found.
Days & hours of operation	Mon.–Sat. 10 AM–7 PM Sun. 10 AM — 6 PM

Description

This urban pet store gets everything right! For such a small space there's an excellent selection of food, dog and cat toys, and pet accessories. They really understand pets' nutritional needs, and organic foods and treats are a specialty. Catnip & Bones has a very "neighborhood" vibe: customers talk with each other and ask the staff for advice. Come here with your dog once, and the second time you and your best friend will be greeted by name. I know a little boy who used to walk his dog several blocks just so he could go in and chat up the staff. They were always happy to see him, interested in what he had to say and what his dog had been up to. That's something you can't buy on the Internet. Pam and her staff help keep dogs happy and their owners connected.

Half Moon Bay Feed & Fuel

Address	331 Main Street Half Moon Bay, CA 94019
Phone	650 726-4814
Website	www.halfmoonbay-feedandfuel.com
Days & hours of operation	Mon.–Fri. 8:30 AM–6 PM Sat. 9 AM–5 PM Sun. 10 AM–4 PM

Description

Situated right on Main Street as you enter the downtown area, this must be the most visited feed supply store in the country. Day-trippers and tourists wander in looking for souvenirs but find a real-live working feed and farm store. This place has been in business since 1911, and since most tourists don't want to take home live crickets or mealworms, the store now carries clothing and gifts along with the hamster food, cattle feed, saddles, and cow bells. So if you're looking for dusters and hats or riding pants and gloves, they've got you covered. T-shirts are here, of course, and bandanas, too. The prices are what you'd expect for feed — farmers are, after all, in business and watching costs. The souvenir prices seem a bit lower than you'd expect from a shop located on the main street of a tourist town.

22

Surplus Stores

Alameda Army Navy Surplus Store

Address	2500 Embarcadero Oakland, CA 94606
Phone	510 261-5152
Website	www.Alamedasurplusstore.com
Days & hours of operation	Tues.–Sat. 10:30 AM–7 PM Sun. 11 AM–5:30 PM

Description

Alameda Army Navy Surplus has moved from Alameda. That's just the first of many changes. This is not like most other surplus stores where goods are piled haphazardly throughout an aging space. No, this is in a fairly new building, and the stock is displayed more or less like any normal retailer. That makes items easy to find and inspect or try on, but some of the "thrill of the hunt" is missing. The knives, bayonets, and swords are here. This is a classic surplus store in a not-so-classic location. This is a good starting point if you're a bargain-hunting camper or if you're putting together an earthquake emergency kit. Those preparing for the end of civilization as we know it should check for supplies here as well. You'll find binoculars for $20, handcuffs for $30, and tents $40. If you want camouflage shirts or pants, they've got you covered there, too.

Berkeley Surplus

Address	1640 San Pablo Avenue Berkeley, CA 94702
Phone	510 524-8434
Website	www.Berkeleysurplus.com
Days & hours of operation	Mon.–Fri. 10 AM–5:30 PM Sat. 10 AM–5 PM Sun. Noon–4 PM

Description

This small store is stuffed with military uniforms from around the world. Need goggles? This place has a huge selection (especially if you're into Steam Punk and Burning Man standup). U.S. WW II Mountain Goggles, never used, with case, $42. Knock-offs of British WWII goggles even come in two styles: Black metal for $32 or chrome for $36. Surplus classics are here, too: Mosquito netting, canteens, and water containers in many shapes and styles. There's a wide selection of military and military-type clothing. Current-issue USN bellbottoms, Battles Dress Pants long and short, plus odd items like C-clamps, ammo boxes, and miner's lamps. Used parachutes are among the store specialties. Made of rip-stop nylon, these 'chutes come in twenty-five and thirty-five-foot diameters, and start at just $40. The more-desired colors will run you $100. This store has been around selling military surplus in Berkeley for over fifty years. The people here know what they're doing and what customers want.

Cal Surplus

Address	1541 Haight Street San Francisco, CA 94117
Phone	415 861-0404
Website	www.Calsurplussf.com
Days & hours of operation	Mon.–Sat. 11 AM–6 PM Sun. Noon–5 PM

Description

This is the surplus store you'd expect to find on Haight Street in San Francisco. Rather than a drab tan building, a bright blue façade greets you, the painting of a lizard and a red-and-yellow sign declaring that the store sells "Urban Surplus" as well as military surplus. There's plenty for the camper to dig through, and those who like hats should definitely check out the selection. Sun hats for the ladies are stacked up next to old-guy vacation hats and cowboy hats that seem to never go out of style. Camping gear is very big here, as are military-issue clothing and work clothes.

Mountain View Surplus

Address	1299 W. El Camino Real Mountain View, CA 94040
Phone	650 646-3546
Website	www.Mvsurplus.com
Days & hours of operation	Mon.–Fri. 10 AM–7 PM Sat. 10 AM–6 PM Sun. 11 AM–5 PM

Description

This medium-sized store has been here forever. Because of that you can find hidden gems like military wear long ago sold out at other stores. I grew up going to this place, pushing my nose up against the window and waiting for the day I could actually afford the two-man rubber raft. My best friend finally got his money together and bought one. We took it to a local lake, blew it up, and paddled out with two little paddles. It floated just fine. Surely these guys have something you're pining away for. This is a great place to shop for earthquake preparedness, some close-to-the-ground camping, and Burning Man. Travel supplies such as duffle bags are cheap and sturdy, and military-issue blankets will keep you warm — if somewhat scratchy.

The Mountain View

Address	2045 S. Bascom Avenue Campbell, CA 95008
Phone	408 377-1362
Website	www.Thearmynavysurplus.com
Days & hours of operation	Mon, Tues. Fri. Sat. 10AM – 6PM Wed. Thur. 10AM – 9PM Sun 11AM – 5PM

Description

The Mountain View has been selling army/navy surplus and more in this same location since 1976. Besides their huge selection of both new and used military clothing and equipment, they also have an extensive collection of camping supplies, plus backpacking and survival gear. You can find sailor hats for $1.99, all-weather boots for $29, and get personalized dog tags for $5.99. New backpacks, good for school or a day hike, go for $11–$45; shoulder bags from $10–$25. You can buy used sleeping bags, which regularly sell for $139, for just $50, with some bags going for less. Need mosquito netting? You can buy it here for $4.99 a yard. They sell full military uniforms for $119, but they also rent them, so if you're thinking of dressing up as a police or military officer for Halloween, you can get a full-dress uniform for $30 — $60, depending on the how many accessories you want.

23

Flea Markets

Alameda Point Antiques Faire

Address	2900 Navy Way Alameda, CA 94501
Phone	510 522-7500
Website	www.alamedapointantiquesfaire.com
Days & hours of operation	First Sunday of every month, 6 AM–3 PM

Description

This is where antique dealers go to get their stuff! This faire is held on the first Sunday of every month. This place is huge, with more than 800 dealer spaces. All items sold here must be at least twenty years old, so there are plenty of antiques and vintage items, but not nearly as much junk as at other outdoor markets dealing in used items. Anyone who's a regular here has a story of the amazing deal he or she got... or the one that got away. The cost of admission is on a sliding scale. The sooner you want in, the more you pay: entry costs $15 at 6:00 AM; $10 at 7:30 AM; $5 at 9:00 AM Entry after 2:00 PM is free, but of course all of the good items have long been snatched up by then.

Berkeley Flea Market

Address	1937 Ashby Avenue Berkeley, CA 94703
Phone	510 644-0744
Website	BerkeleyFleaMarket.com
Days & hours of operation	Sat.–Sun. 7 AM–7 PM

Description

This is a classic flea market with a Berkeley flair. There are plenty of the usual car stereos and tools, and along with those items there are natural foods, New-Age music, and incense. Rasta items, books, and original arts and crafts round out the offerings. Look for tie-dye, too — lots of tie-dye.

Napa Really Really Free Market

Address	Veterans Memorial Park
Phone	No number found
Website	www.reallyreallyfree.org
Days & hours of operation	Noon, the last Sunday of every month

Description

This is part of an international movement of open-air markets called "Really Really Free Market"(RRFM), which require "No Money. No Barter. No Trade. Everything is Free." The idea is for participants to bring what they don't need and give it away. It's described as being like a potluck dinner where you contribute what you can — goods, skills, a nice disposition — and take what you need. The basic theory is that there's already enough stuff available for everyone if only we, as a community, share. There's also a RRFM held at Deloris Park in San Francisco on the last Saturday of every month.

The San Jose Flea Market

Address	1590 Berryessa Rd. San Jose, CA 95133
Phone	408 453-1110
Website	www.sjfm.com
Days & hours of operation	Wed.–Fri. 6 AM–dusk; Sat.–Sun. 5 AM–dusk

Description

This is the big daddy of flea markets! On a slow week-day there are 200 vendors. On a Sunday there can be 1,500! It's huge and has been in operation since 1960. There are still plenty of used items for sale here as well as new and used clothing, furniture, jewelry, and sports memorabilia. Knock-off purses and watches can be had if you know where to ask — and asking around is easy. These days there are groceries of all kinds, including fresh and exotic vegetables. There are plenty of restaurants too, and the food is great. I bought the best burrito I've ever eaten here. The place can really get crowded since many locals do the weekly shopping here, using it as an outdoor mall. Admission is $2, but that's waived if you pay $5 for parking.

Treasure Island Flea

Address	Avenue of the Palms San Francisco, CA 94130
Phone	415 989-0245
Website	www.TreasureIslandFlea.com
Days & hours of operation	Sat.–Sun. the last full weekend of every month, 10 AM–4 PM

Description

If there's a finer, more vibrant flea market than this, I'd love to see it. Located on the grass area overlooking the bay and San Francisco, this has the feel of a community celebration. Local musicians, artists, and craftspeople compete for your attention. Some of the city's best food trucks are set up, and there are California wines for sale as well. There are activities for the kids, and DIY seminars are held. Many of the items you'd expect at a flea market are for sale here, but there are also amazing antiques and crafts you won't see anywhere else. It's easy to get here on public transportation. Tourists should consider spending an hour or so here. Admission is $3 for adults; kids are admitted free. It's worth the price for the view alone.

24

Outlet Malls

American Tin Cannery

Address	125 Ocean View Blvd. Pacific Grove, CA 93950
Phone	831 372-1442
Website	www.Americantincannery.com
Days & hours of operation	Mon.–Sun. 10 AM–6 PM

Description

This place is a combination of a touristy shopping plaza and an outlet mall. The twenty-two stores include outlet mainstays like Bass, Pendleton, Van Heusen, Izod and Reebok-Rockport, but local stores, a miniature-golf course, and a boxing gym are mixed in.

Factory Stores at the Y

Address	At the Y, Highways 50 and 89 South Lake Tahoe, CA 96150
Phone	530 544-2322
Website	www.shopthey.com
Days & hours of operation	Mon.–Sun. 10 am–6 pm

Description

Factory Stores at the Y is so named because it sits at Tahoe's famous "Y" intersection. It's a small mall, with just eleven stores, but it does have Bass, Adidas, Van Heusen, and Izod outlets. Summer sales are especially good here.

Folsom Premium Outlets

Address	13000 Folsom Blvd. Folsom, CA 95630
Phone	916 985-0312
Website	www.premiumoutlets.com/outlets/ outlet.asp?id=2
Days & hours of operation	Regular Mon.–Sat. 10 AM–9 PM Sun. 10 AM–6 PM Check the website for special sale and holiday hours.

Description

Folsom Premium Outlets is located between Sacramento and Lake Tahoe/Reno. The outlet has eighty stores including Nautica, Saks Fifth Avenue Off 5th, Banana Republic, Guess, Wilsons Leather, and Tommy Hilfiger.

Gilroy Premium Outlets

Address	681 Leavesley Road Gilroy, CA 95020
Phone	408 842-3729
Website	www.premiumoutlets.com/outlets/ outlet.asp?id=23
Days & hours of operation	Regular Mon.–Sat. 10 AM–9 PM Sun. 10 AM–6 PM Check the website for special sale and holiday hours.

Description

Gilroy Premium Outlets is located south of San Jose. It's a gigantic strip mall-type place, with 145 stores, so it can take quite a while to see everything. All the big names are here including Hugo Boss, Lucky Brand, and Polo Ralph Lauren.

Great Mall

Address	447 Great Mall Drive Milpitas, CA 95035
Phone	408 945-4022
Website	simon.com/Mall/?id=1250
Days & hours of operation	Regular Mon.–Sat. 10 AM–9 PM Sun. 11 AM–8 PM Check the website for special sale and holiday hours.

Description

The Great Mall is a combo of a giant indoor shopping mall and an outlet center. There are over 200 stores, with new ones moving in all the time. A new addition is New York and Company, which joins Neiman Marcus Last Call and the Vans Shoe Outlet. Also in the mix: Forever 21 and H&M.

Marina Square Center

Address	1201 Marina Blvd. San Leandro, CA 94577
Phone	510 347-3010
Website	www.marinasquarecenter.com
Days & hours of operation	Regular Mon.–Sat. 10 AM–9 PM Sun. 11 AM–6 PM Check the website for special sale and holiday hours.

Description

Location, location, location is what makes this mall unique. Marina Square Center is a cross between a little outlet mall and a littler strip mall. There are more than a dozen outlet stores, including a Converse Outlet, a GUESS Factory Store, a NIKE Clearance Store, a Nordstrom Rack, and a Gymboree Outlet, and lots of restaurants.

Napa Premium Outlets

Address	629 Factory Stores Drive Napa, CA 94558
Phone	707 224-2489
Website	premiumoutlets.com/outlets/outlet.asp?id=25
Days & hours of operation	Regular Mon.–Thurs. 10 AM–8 PM Fri.–Sat. 10 AM–9 PM Sun. 10 AM–7 PM Check the website for special sale and holiday hours.

Description

This is a great stop when you're heading into wine country. Most of the big names are here, including Calvin Klein, Coach, and Cole Haan.

Petaluma Village Premium

Address	200 Petaluma Blvd. North Petaluma, CA 94952
Phone	707 778-9300
Website	www.premiumoutlets.com/outlets/ outlet.asp?id=24
Days & hours of operation	Regular Mon.–Thurs. 10 AM–8 PM Fri.–Sat. 10 AM–9:0 PM Sun. 10 AM–7 PM Check the website for special sale and holiday hours.

Description

Petaluma Village Premium Outlets is north of San Francisco. There are about sixty stores, including Puma and Nine West Outlet.

Tracy Outlets

Address	1005 East Pescadero Avenue Tracy, CA 95304
Phone	209 833-1895
Website	www.mytracyoutlets.com
Days & hours of operation	Mall Mon.–Sat. 10 AM–8 PM Sun. 11 AM–6 PM

Description

Tracy Outlets is a smaller outlet mall with only about twenty stores. Still, many of the big players are located here, including Carters Children's Wear, Casual Male, Levi's, Gap, and Lane Bryant.

Vacaville Premium Outlets

Address	321 Nut Tree Road Vacaville, CA 95687
Phone	707 447-5755
Website	premiumoutlets.com/outlets/outlet. asp?id=50
Days & hours of operation	Regular Mon–Sat. 10 AM–9 PM Sun. 10 AM–6 PM Check the website for special sale and holiday hours.

Description

Vacaville Premium Outlets are located between San Francisco and Sacramento. There are 120 stores, many are upscale brands like Burberry, Calvin Klein, and Coach.

25

Food and Beverages

City Beer Store

Address	1168 Folsom Street, Suite 101 San Francisco, CA 94103
Phone	415 503-1033
Website	www.citybeerstore.com
Days & hours of operation	Tues.–Sat. Noon to 10 PM Sun. Noon to 6 PM

Description

If you like beer, city life, and lofts, this is the place for you. Just walking into the store is amazing; a tasting room to the right and a wall of cold beer to the left. Hmm... where to begin? This is a beer store and tasting room that is actively used as a fun neighborhood bar. Open for more than six years now, here is proof that fine beer is just as important — and fun — as fine wines. City Beer offers more than 300 beers and ales in bottles and on tap. Buying here offers huge savings because you never get trapped into buying a beer you don't like. In most stores you have to invest in an entire six-pack to find out if you like a particular brew. That might not sound like much, but when you're talking about beers that cost between $6 and $20, that's a lot of dough. Not to mention the effort you have to go through pawning off the beer you don't like to friends when they visit. At City Beer you are encouraged to mix and match. If that still seems like too much of an investment, grab a beer, go to the bar, and enjoy it on premises. Dating tip: This place is packed with young men. If you like to meet young men, go here.

Earthgrains-Rainbo Baking Company

Address	955 Kennedy Street Oakland, CA 94606
Phone	510 436-5350
Website	No working website found.
Days & hours of operation	Mon – Fri 8AM – 5:30PM Sat 9AM – 5:30PM

Description

This store is right off 880 in Oakland near Alameda. The store is located at the bakery, so you know the items here are fresh. Bread sells for half what you pay in retail stores, and there are also deals on Little Debbie products: donuts sell for 75 cents, and two brownies go for $1. Throughout the Bay Area, Nemo's muffins are sold for $1.50; here you can pick them up for 79 cents. Check in often, as other grocery items are available for a while and then gone. Local overstocks end up here, too: on a recent visit, candy bars were selling for half off, and there were deals on condiments such as mustard, and off-brand items like peanut butter.

Entenmann's – Oroweat Bakery Outlet

Address	264 S. Spruce Avenue South San Francisco, CA 94080
Phone	650 952-8372
Website	www.bimbobakeriesusa.com
Days & hours of operation	Mon.–Fri. 10 AM–6 PM Sat. 10 AM–4 PM

Description

Calling this a day-old bread place doesn't do it justice. The parent company is Bimbo Bakeries, which owns a dozen of the most important bakeries in the nation: Thomas' English Muffins, Tia Rosa, Entenmann's, and Francisco are just a few of the brand names you know. Not everything they bake is for sale at their outlets, but most of it is available. Want bagels? Buy a bag for $1. They have fresh-baked loaves of bread for $2, with is nearly half of what I pay at the local supermarket. If you're willing to go day-old, prices drop to about a third of what you'd expect to pay elsewhere. There are daily specials and a few non-bakery items. The best deals and freshest breads are available Wednesdays and Sundays. There are discounts for seniors, too. There are half a dozen stores in the greater Bay Area, but they aren't all exactly easy to find or centrally located, so stock up and stash some items in the freezer. To get the very best deal, ask for a Loyalty Card. Spend $25 and they'll give you two free items of your choosing.

Ghirardelli Factory Store

Address	1111 139th Avenue San Leandro, CA 94578
Phone	510 346-3146
Website	www.Ghirardelli.com
Days & hours of operation	Mon.–Fri. 9:30 AM–5:30 PM Sat. 9:30 AM–5 PM Sun. 10 AM–5 PM

Description

This store is exactly where it should be — and where you'd least expect it. The factory is in an industrial area deep in San Leandro. Finding it can be a challenge, so use a GPS or just follow your nose. The aroma is amazing and makes the shopping experience unlike any other. The store is the size of an old-fashioned candy store, but it's packed with chocolate and Ghirardelli products. You can't take a step without finding yet another great deal. The biggest savings come with seasonal items, like Christmas chocolates in January, or Valentine's Day chocolates in March. Those who grew up in the San Francisco Bay Area in the 1970s and '80s remember Ghirardelli best for the tubes of chocolate discs called Flicks that they used to buy in convenience stores and at candy counters. The company no longer calls them Flicks, and the tubes are gone, but the discs are sold here in plastic bags. The secret to getting the very best deal is to buy a canvas Ghirardelli tote for $6. If you have a tote with you when you shop here, everything is 15% off.

Golden Gate Fortune Cookies

Address	56 Ross Alley San Francisco, CA 94108
Phone	415 781-3956
Website	No working website found.
Days & hours of operation	Mon.–Sun. 9 AM–6 PM

Description

If you grew up in San Francisco and weren't brought here on a field trip with your elementary school class, I believe you have the right to file a lawsuit. If you weren't lucky enough to live here during your early school years, then go now — it's never too late to have a happy childhood. Located in a tiny Chinatown alley in a very small storefront, this place is living history; it's San Francisco's version (and a much cooler version, I might add) of Colonial Williamsburg. The people working here dress strangely and operate ancient machinery. However, this place is for real. They make and sell fortune cookies here. Inside you'll find two women taking warm fortune cookies off a conveyer belt, quickly folding them, and inserting the fortune. You can even write your own fortune for them to insert into a cookie for you to take home. Be nice and you'll be offered a free sample, pre-folded. A bag of six fortune cookies costs $1; a big bag goes for $4.25. Often you'll be given a few extra for free. The cookies come in two flavors: regular and chocolate. Taking a picture of the ladies costs 50¢.

Hostess Bakery Outlet

Address	1946 23rd Street San Pablo, CA 94806
Phone	510 215-5736
Website	www.Hostessbrands.com
Days & hours of operation	Mon.–Fri. 8:30 AM–5 PM Sat. 10 AM–5 PM

Description

There are eight other Bay Area locations.

If you like Ho-Hos or cream-filled cupcakes, this is your one-stop shop for inexpensive bakery goods. There are many half-price deals, not only on Hostess products but also on Wonder Bread, Dolly Madison treats, and a wide variety of Nature's Pride items. Most are about half off on a daily basis, and sales are common. This is great place to stop on the way to soccer games when it's your turn to provide the after-game treat. Before you go to the duck pond, stop here for day-old bread. Hostess/Wonder have stores circling the bay area, and some — in unusual and older shopping districts and faded mini-malls — might seem a bit scary, but low rents is one of the ways they keep the prices so low. Don't let the locations scare you away from getting a deal. The folks working here are the best and will go out of their way to help you find items that aren't readily apparent.

It's-It Ice Cream Outlet

Address	304 Spring Street Suisun City, CA 94585
Phone	707 425-1900
Website	www.Facebook.com/pages/its-it-outlet
Days & hours of operation	Tues.–Sat. 11 AM–6 PM Sun. in summer: 11 AM–4 PM

Description

You'll find the original IT'S-IT ice-cream treat here, and at a great price. For those not familiar with this delicacy, an IT'S-IT is a scoop of ice cream sandwiched between two oatmeal cookies, and the sandwich is then dipped in dark chocolate. First created at San Francisco's Playland By The Sea in 1928, they're now made in Burlingame. So why is the outlet located in the Suisun City waterfront district? This is where they bake the cookies. IT'S-IT sandwiches sell for $1.25 here, but drop to 83 cents if you buy a dozen. You can mix and match flavors, from the original vanilla to mint, cappuccino, and chocolate. You can also purchase Stella's Gourmet Cookie Dough (the IT'S IT dough). For $9 you get four dozen cookies' worth. Flavors include the original oatmeal, chocolate chip, peanut butter, and others. The last time I was here, a skateboarder walked into the store and announced he had just been released from county jail. This was his very first stop after release. They sell other ice-cream treats here, too, including the Big Daddy, Super Sundae, and Chips IT.

Jackson Market

Address	1201 Jackson Street San Francisco, CA 94109
Phone	415 474-4861
Website	www.jacksonmarket.com
Days & hours of operation	Mon. — Sat. 9:30 AM–6 PM Sun. Noon –5 PM

Description

This market isn't easy to get to. Jackson is sometimes a two-way street running east to west, but in some areas it runs one-way from west to east, and in others, it runs one-way in the opposite direction, east to west. You'll find this little market at the corner of Jones Street. A true corner market, it carries the daily staples: milk, bread, lunchmeats, and soft drinks. It also hides a secret: This gem of a store makes some of the best beef jerky. Go inside and you see no signs or displays touting it. You feel like you're in some kind of beef jerky speakeasy. You glance around, and then ask for beef jerky. The counter help, most likely a family member or a friend of the family, whips it out from below the counter. Five ounces in a stapled plastic bag for $8., or a half-pound vacuum packed bag for $11. Buy one of each — one for now, one for later. The jerky has no preservatives or MSG. It has a different taste, a little sweeter than most, which makes it pair well with movies or hanging out on courtroom stairs waiting for the verdict (just ask any news crew in the know).

Lucca Ravioli Company

Address	1100 Valencia Street San Francisco, CA 94110
Phone	415 647-5581
Website	www.Luccaravioli.com
Days & hours of operation	Mon.–Sat. 9 AM–6 PM

Description

This is an old-time favorite for San Franciscans buying Italian food products. The display counter is filled with fresh Italian meats, cheeses, pastas, and sauces. The selection alone would be worth the trip, but the prices here are excellent, too. My friend Dominic turned me on to this place. He drives across town, passing up a couple of other delis on the way. He says, "This is the freshest, best-priced Italian anywhere." I don't argue about Italian food with guys named Dominic. A true deli, you can run in and get a quick sandwich or take your time and figure out your next Italian dinner. As the name would imply, ravioli is the specialty: Cheese, spinach, beef and, during the holidays, turkey ravioli, are made fresh in their kitchen. Pair the ravioli (or other pastas) with a house-made meat, marinara, pesto, or cream sauce, and you're good to go. This is an authentic big-city deli experience with much to see, wonderful accents and speech patterns to admire, and aromas to die for.

Otis Spunkmeyer Factory Store

Address	14490 Catalina Street San Leandro, CA 94577
Phone	510 667-6103
Website	www.Spunkmeyer.com
Days & hours of operation	Mon.–Fri. 9 AM–5 PM

Description

A true factory outlet, this cookie and baked-goods store is located right at the factory in Hayward. Stepping out of your car and into the envelope of cookie aroma is a wonderful experience. The store itself is very small, which gives it a cozy, friendly feel, kind of like a break room for a factory, which I believe it doubles as. All the Spunkmeyer products are on sale here: muffins, brownies bagels, Danish, and loaf cakes. The cookies are fresh baked, but don't try to get one by yourself — this is not a self-serve operation. The cookies are warm from the oven and more than reasonably priced at only 49 cents each. They're even cheaper in bulk: three cookies go for $1.35, and a dozen for $4.50. There's an additional discount if you phone in an order for five dozen or more. Think in terms of school dances and snack time after Little League games. Bagels are a steal at 75 cents and come in two flavors: plain and cinnamon-raisin. All the pricing is right, but the best deal is cookie dough: one pound is only $3.50, or save a bundle buying in bulk: 20 pounds of cookie dough costs just $49.50.

Peerless Coffee & Tea

Address	260 Oak Street Oakland, CA 94607
Phone	510 763-1763
Website	www.peerlesscoffee.com
Days & hours of operation	Mon.–Fri. 8:30 AM–5:30 PM Sat. 9 AM–5 PM

Description

This family-owned company has been roasting coffee since 1924. This is the company store, and it sells the latest coffees and teas the company offers. That, however, is not why they're included in this book. The coffee and teas are great, and the staff here knows how to brew great coffee, but one very good reason for showing up here has nothing to do with beverages. Peerless also sells fresh-roasted peanuts. It seems only old-timers and TV news crews know about that, even though it says PEANUTS on the front of the building. The peanuts come in the shell either salted or unsalted. They're fresh and are kept warm, and a one-pound bag costs just $2.85, so stop here on your way to the big game.

See's Candies
Quantity Discount Shop

Address	400 S. Airport Blvd. South San Francisco, CA 94080
Phone	650 583-6349
Website	www.sees.com
Days & hours of operation	Mon.–Fri. 10 AM–6 PM Sat. 10 AM–5 PM

Description

Six locations throughout the greater Bay Area

See's has been a Bay Area favorite since the first store opened here in 1936. This location still sells candy by the piece, but it's really set up for bigger purchases. Businesses that buy fifty pounds get discounts up to 22%. The more they buy the deeper the discount. You don't have to be a big spender to get the same deal. See's has a program that allows all employees of a bulk-purchasing businesses to get the discount. I recently went in and asked if the parent corporation of Channel 7 had bought enough candy for me to get a deal. The answer was yes! A pound of my favorites would now be marked down about 20%, a savings of more than $3 per box. If your company doesn't buy in bulk, you and your friends can band together and do it.

TCHO Factory

Address	Pier 17 The Embarcadero San Francisco, CA 94111
Phone	Main: 415 981-0189 Tours: 415 963-5090
Website	www.tcho.com
Days & hours of operation	Mon. — Fri. 9 AM–5:30 PM Sat. — Sun. 1 PM–5:30 PM

Description

Who says manufacturing is dead in the United States? Here's a factory located on some of the most expensive real estate in the country: Pier 17, The Embarcadero. Just down the street from Pier 39, this place is a secret hiding in plain sight, but it will certainly turn into a huge tourist attraction. Beat the crowds by going now. You can buy some of the best of a new wave of chocolates being created by artisans who use only the best ingredients. What makes the chocolate even better is that it's made with cacao beans from growers who are called partners and who receive help applying sustainable techniques. TCHO calls this the New American Chocolate. You will call it out of this world. The best way to get a deal here is to take the tour. There are two tours daily, at 10:30 AM and 2:00 PM To guarantee a spot it's best to sign up online in advance. After the tour there will be a free tasting. Ask for the 10% off coupon.

The Nut Factory

Address	3477 Golden Gate Way Lafayette, CA 94549
Phone	925 283-6151
Website	www.theoriginalnutfactory.com
Days & hours of operation	Mon.–Fri. 9 AM–5 PM Sat. 10 AM–3 PM

Description

The Nut Factory is tucked away on a back street in an area you wouldn't be likely to wander down, but there's a reason to search it out. They've been selling quality fresh-roasted nuts in downtown Lafayette for over fifty years. To insure freshness, they roast the nuts in small batches, using their unique wet-roasting technique, as opposed to the typical dry-roast method. These guys aren't the cheapest you'll find, but they're among the best. Don't let the name fool you, either — The Nut Factory sells more than just nuts. They're known for their quality candies, cookies, jams, and other gourmet food items, which they pack in made-to-order gift baskets. To gear up for the holiday gift-basket season each year, the Nut Factory opens up its back factory area on the last Thursday and Saturday of October so customers can enjoy free samples of the latest delicious offerings. They serve up great chocolates, too, but not during the summer. Why? I'm told the building's not air conditioned, and it would be a sticky mess.

The Wine Club

Address	953 Harrison Street San Francisco, CA 94107
Phone	415 512-9086
Website	www.thewineclub.com
Days & hours of operation	Mon.–Sat. 10 AM–7 PM Sun. 10 AM–6 PM

Description

Also in San Jose

Back in the day, many stores were called Club; for instance, Price Club, or Pet Club. I don't know why — I guess they thought we all wanted to join a club without actually, you know, joining a club. Well, Wine Club is that kind of club. Sure, they offer a club that'll send you wine if you wish, but you don't have to join to get into this store and buy some of the best-priced wines in the country. There's a huge selection at wonderful prices, and you'll often have the store all to yourself. Why? I think the name scares some people away. Wine. Club. Snooty. Don't be a scaredy-cat. This place is packed with a great selection of modestly priced wines. Want to spend less than $10 a bottle? They've got you covered. Want to spend a couple hundred to impress someone? They have that, too. I bought Cakebread Chardonnay here once for ten bucks less than anywhere else. It was still $40, but for that year, a steal. The people who work here are easygoing and knowledgeable, and they make wine accessible. If you really want to get into it, they offer wine-storage lockers for under $30 a month, and a real club — but don't get me started.

Wine.com Outlet

Address	2220 4th Street Berkeley, CA 94710
Phone	510 704-8007
Website	www.wine.com
Days & hours of operation	Tues.–Sat. 11 AM–5 PM

Description

These are the big boys and girls in online wine sales. Good pricing, education, and man, they keep track of the "wine points," that's for sure. This is the outlet store for their online operation, located next to a huge warehouse where 2,500 wines are stored and ready for shipping. In the outlet itself are more than 350 wines set up on racks. The staff is helpful, and there are kiosks in the back of the store so you can access the wines in the warehouse. Wine.com does a brisk business in gift baskets, and with good reason: Unlike many baskets offered in Napa and Sonoma, these actually have nice wines and good pairings that are thoughtfully designed and offer savings. For less than $30 you can get a sparkling wine and Godiva chocolate gift set. It's price points like that, that make their gift-basket sales so healthy. The store itself is clean and well lighted, but oddly enough there's no wine tasting there.

26

Services

AW Collision Group

Address	435 Serramonte Blvd. Colma, CA 94014
Phone	650 992-1400
Website	www.AWCollision.com
Days & hours of operation	Mon.–Fri. 7:30 AM– 6 PM Sat. 9 AM–2 PM

Description

Six locations throughout the Greater Bay Area

Autowest Collision Group has been in business for over twenty-five years. They have collision centers throughout California, and are now expanding eastward with one in Las Vegas. This is one of the nation's fastest-growing privately held collision-center chains. The work performed here is of the highest quality, which is apparent when you drive up and see rows of high-end cars being repaired. These are picky owners who want the job done right. The team at AW Collision is all about customer service. In today's world, a major part of a repair shop's job is to negotiate with and even fight with your auto-insurance company — just like your doctor does with your health insurer. The team here doesn't hesitate, going to bat for their clients to get the work done correctly. They offer a lifetime warranty on all labor, and a one-year manufacturer's warranty on parts.

Bertolli's Auto Body

Address	1345 East Francisco Blvd. San Rafael, CA 94901
Phone	Tel: 415 456-1992
Website	www.bertollis.com
Days & hours of operation	Mon.–Fri. 8 AM–5 PM

Description

Bertolli's Auto Body has been around for decades. Started by Frank Bertolli, the shop is now owned and operated by his daughter Laura. This is one of the few body shops in the United States that's owned by a woman. Bertolli's is known for taking a stand on consumer rights. I first met Laura when she was working with a local lawmaker to protect customers' auto-repair rights. Bertolli's does a big business in custom paintjobs, and offers a lifetime guarantee on labor and a one-year warranty (from supplier) on parts. Ask for details.

Collectible Coins & Jewelry

Address	226 Shoreline Highway Mill Valley, CA 94941
Phone	415 381-6340
Website	www.Goldexchangemarin.com
Days & hours of operation	Mon.–Fri. 10 AM–4 PM Sat. 11 AM–1 PM

Description

When you arrive at this address you find a gray building that has seen better days. At the door there's a button you push to be buzzed in. You walk inside and there's a glass counter display case with jewelry and coins. Behind it is the proprietor, Carter Collins, with his scales and a huge safe. This looks like a gold-buying and selling operation out of a Western movie. I sent an undercover production assistant into this store when I was researching a TV report on buying and selling gold. I didn't know what to expect. What we got was a friendly, well-intentioned offer that came out exactly as it should have. Since then I've spoken with several other customers, all of them happy with their transactions.

Dick's Antennas

Address	6389 El Paseo Drive San Jose, CA 95120
Phone	408 268-6814
Website	No working website found.
Days & hours of operation	Call for appointment

Description

I met Dick when I was doing a report on over-the-air TV. The industry was making the switch to digital TV, and that got me thinking about antennas. I figured there wouldn't be any professionals left in the field. I was wrong. Dick was my go-to guy, and I found happy customers and a whole new antenna setup. They are now flat and square with a metal grid. If you're fortunate enough to live in a good coverage area, you can pick up a lot of free TV channels and even a free viewer guide off air. Dick makes it all possible by rigging the antenna so it actually works. He's a good guy and his service is bargain priced.

Famous Wayne's Shoe Shine

Address	Foot of California Street at the Cable Car Turnaround San Francisco, CA 94101
Phone	No phone
Website	No working website found.
Days & hours of operation	Weekdays when it isn't raining.

Description

In this part of the city, Famous Wayne is the go-to guy for a shine. Outside on the sidewalk and seated up high where you can get a view of your surroundings, this is what city life and good grooming are all about. Wayne or his helper will make sure your shoes are cleaned, shined, and ready for your meeting. Wayne charges $8 for a shine, but you can buy a card that offers 25 shines for $50. There's also a "Good for Lifetime" card that goes for $300. That price is negotiable.

National Gown Cleaners

Address	625 McGlincey Lane Campbell, CA 95008
Phone	408 371-3174
Website	www.NationalGown.com
Days & hours of operation	Mon. Wed. Fri. 9 AM — 5 PM

Description

Don't let the location — in a cinderblock industrial building located next to an auto-glass company — scare you away. Brides from all over the world use this service. It's also the place where cleaners who ruin gowns send them for repair. National Gown Cleaners has been in the textile business for over eighty years and now specialize in preserving gowns for future generations. The gowns are returned to near-new condition, cleaned, and properly boxed for long-term storage. National Gown claims its preserved gowns to be of museum quality, and museums do use them as a resource. Prices can vary widely, depending on how much work is needed, but preserving the average bridal gown costs between $175 and $425. Hey, if you wore Grandmother's dress at your wedding, it's worth the expense to make it available for your granddaughter.

Pacific Precious Metals

Address	302 Caledonia Street Suite 3 (2nd Floor) Sausalito, CA 94965
Phone	415 877-1791
Website	www.Pacificpreciousemetals.com
Days & hours of operation	Mon.–Fri. 10 AM–5:30 PM Sat. 10 AM–4 PM

Description

With the price of gold and silver hitting new highs, consumers have started to cash in their old gold jewelry and the silverware they're not using. I went undercover to see what prices I'd be offered, and that's how I found this place. I sent in a producer who brought along a few items in different grades of gold. She was treated fairly and got a good price for it, about 80% of the spot price, which was the correct payment for that amount of gold. Dan Barrett owns the place and runs it like a financial service company. Good for him — and you!

Square Trade

Address	Internet and phone only
Phone	877-927-7268
Website	Squaretrade.com
Days & hours of operation	24 / 7

Description

Square Trade is an aftermarket warranty company. If you buy something electronic and want a warranty, you can buy it at the store where you shopped or maybe the manufacturer or at a third-party warranty company like Square Trade. Based in San Francisco, Square Trade offers many warranties at half what others charge. The standard warranty covers all mechanical and electrical failures that might occur during normal use. You get 100% parts and labor coverage with zero deductible. An iPhone warranty costs $99; eReader warranties sell for $19. Both come with protection against accidents.

The Tix Booth

Address	350 Powell Street Union Square San Francisco, CA
Phone	415 433-7827
Website	www.tixbayarea.com
Days & hours of operation	Tue. – Sat 11AM – 5PM, Sun. 10AM – 3PM

Description

The TIX booth offers full-price and discount tickets to nearly every arts and cultural event in the greater Bay Area. The real prizes here, though, are the deeply discounted same-day tickets to some of the best theater in the area. Check here before you buy direct from the theater or other venue. For every ticket purchased through TIX, a large portion of the service charge you pay goes to Theatre Bay Area, a nonprofit charitable organization that supports classes, grants, auditions, and health support for thousands of Bay Area artists and arts professionals.

27

Entertainment

Children's Fairyland

Address	699 Bellevue Avenue Oakland, CA 94610
Phone	510 238-6876
Website	www.fairyland.org
Days & hours of operation	Hours change by season, so check before planning your trip.

Description

Children's Fairyland has been entertaining and amazing children since 1950. For one low price you can spend the day at the ten-acre facility, checking out the storybook sets, gentle rides, and friendly animals. The live entertainment includes puppet shows, storytelling, and theater productions, making this one magical spot in the Oakland Hills. Most amusement parks are costly enough that families have to plan in advance and make sacrifices to attend. Not here: Infants are admitted free, everyone else, age one to 101, $8. There are special deals for field trips, and they offer day camps during the summer months.

Impact Theater

Address	1834 Euclid Avenue Berkeley, CA 94709
Phone	510 224-5744
Website	www.impacttheatre.com
Days & hours of operation	Check showtimes

Description

Impact Theater's tag line says it all: Pizza. Beer. Plays. Talk about accessible theater! This company offers never-before-seen plays written by many local artists, as well as reinterpretations of other more prominent works, like setting Shakespeare in Hollywood. The low prices (general admission tickets sell for $17 in advance, $20 at the door), the pizza, and the beer are what make this so great. In the famous La Val's Subterranean, you order your pizza and beer to go, and then walk down into the basement with your food and take in a play. A cheap date night for sure, and you're supporting the local arts — while eating pizza.

Unfortunately, La Val's Subterranean is not accessible to people in wheelchairs or for whom a flight of stairs is prohibitive. They'd love to be in an accessible venue that's closer to BART and other public transit. If you'd like to help them reach that goal, you might consider making a tax-deductible donation.

Musee Mecanique

Address	Pier 45, Shed A (end of Taylor at Fisherman's Wharf) San Francisco, CA 94133
Phone	415 346-2000
Website	www.Museemechaniquesf.com
Days & hours of operation	Mon.–Fri. 10 AM–7 PM Sat.–Sun. and Holidays, 10 AM 8 PM

Description

Want to know what the world of gaming and entertainment was like before there was Angry Birds, Xbox, even before Atari and Pong? Musee Mecanique (Mechanical Museum) has your answer. A for-profit museum, Musee Mecanique has one of the world's largest collections of antique arcade machines. This place used to creep me out when it was located in the basement of the Cliff House, but now that it has moved it seems much less scary. There are over 200 coin-operated games and wonders, including mechanical boxing matches, fortunetellers, jazz bands, and sex-appeal meters. Some of these items date back to the 1800s, but there are also pinball games from the last half of the 20th century and new(er) video games. There are a couple of old-time photo booths, as well as Skee-Ball and Whack-A-Mole. Along with the games is an assortment of memorabilia, including the world's only known steam-powered motorcycle and the real Laffing Sal from the Fun House at the old Playland by the Beach. Entry is free, but operating the machines will cost you, so bring quarters.

Pacific Pinball Museum

Address	1510 Webster Street Alameda, CA 94501
Phone	510 769-1349
Website	www.pacificpinball.org
Days & hours of operation	Tues.–Thurs. 2 PM–9 PM Fri.–Sat. 11 AM–Midnight; Sun. 11 AM–9 PM

Description

The Pacific Pinball Museum is a nonprofit organization dedicated to teaching science, art, and history through pinball, and to the promotion and preservation of one of America's great pastimes. The museum has a collection of ninety fully playable, historic pinball machines. Now this is where you come in: For an entry fee of $15 for adults and $7.50 for kids under twelve, you get into the museum for the entire day, and can play any machine for as long as you want without sliding a single quarter into a slot. This is truly bargain entertainment, and it's a way of showing your kids that some games take actual physical fitness to play. If you're really into it, there are tournaments to compete in. If you're throwing a birthday party, they've got rooms and deals for that too. Social media startups/companies take note: PPM also has a vintage aluminum trailer that they'll bring to your site and set up for an unforgettable experience.

Playland Not-At-The-Beach

Address	10979 San Pablo Avenue El Cerrito, CA 94530
Phone	510 592-3002
Website	www.playland-not-at-the-beach.org
Days & hours of operation	Sat.–Sun. 10 AM–5 PM

Description

A nonprofit museum dedicated to Playland at the Beach in San Francisco. The landmark shut down in the 1970s, and these people are keeping the memory alive with displays, education, and a whole bunch of fun. There are no rides here, but there are more than thirty free-play pinball machines, video and arcade games, as well as carnival games of skill where you can win prizes. Along with all the fun they offer historic displays like a hand-carved circus and photos and information on the Ocean Beach attractions of the 20th century. They host parties for senior citizens, toddlers, and everyone in-between, great for birthday parties and other gatherings. Entry is $10 for seniors and kids up to fourteen. All others pay $15. Kids three and under are not encouraged to attend.

Push

Address	Venues throughout the Bay Area
Phone	No Number Available
Website	www.RockWithPush.com
Days & hours of operation	Check website for dates and times

Description

This band promises to deliver "classic rock and original roll," and pulls it off big-time. Push is now making the rounds as one of the hottest new bands in the Bay Area. A tip-off that you're watching something different comes when you notice the front man seems a little familiar, like maybe you've seen him before in a different time and place. You have, he's Dan Ashley the long time anchor at ABC 7 News. The band covers classics like Tom Petty's *Mary Jane's Last Dance* and The Rolling Stones' *Jumpin' Jack Flash,* but this is not just a cover band. Push has released its own CD and is building a following because of its own unique style. Who knew being one the sharpest, most studied newsmen in America would prepare you for being a rock and roll phenom?

Santa Cruz Beach Boardwalk

Address	On the beach
Phone	831 460-3342
Website	www.beachboardwalk.com
Days & hours of operation	Mon.–Tues. 9 AM–Midnight Wed.–Thurs. 9 AM–11 PM Fri.–Sat. 9 AM–1 AM Sun. 9 AM–11 PM

Description

It's hard to miss this place if you're in Santa Cruz, but easy to forget to visit because it's always here. This is a great deal for families, since you only pay for what you buy. The teens will want an all-day ride pass for $29; little ones will do well with buying rides one by one. They cost between $3 and $5. Mom and Dad can just stroll along not paying a dime. The boardwalk attractions, like Laser Tag, Mini-Golf, Fright Walk, and Climb 'N Conquer, cost $5 each and aren't included in the ride passes. Parking is free. There are season tickets and special deals for groups. During the summer there are free concerts on Friday nights. Among the bands this past season were Bay Area favorites Eddie Money and Papa Do Run Run. On Wednesdays, movies are shown on the beach; this past year they hit a homerun by showing *Lost Boys,* a movie about teenage vampires in Santa Cruz.

The Mystery Spot

Address	465 Mystery Spot Road Santa Cruz, CA 95065
Phone	831 423-8897
Website	www.mysteryspot.com
Days & hours of operation	Summer Mon.–Fri. 10 AM–6 PM Sat.–Sun. 9 AM–7 PM

Description

You've seen the bumper sticker, now visit the attraction. Like something out of a 1950s family road trip, The Mystery Spot thrives. It appeared to be in danger of closing a couple decades back; now it's a hipster must-see. So what is The Mystery Spot, aside from a place to buy the famous bumper sticker? Well, here's what the people there say: "The Mystery Spot is a gravitational anomaly located in the redwood forests just outside of Santa Cruz, California. It is a circular area of effect around 150 feet or 46 meters in diameter. Within The Mystery Spot you will be stunned as your perceptions of the laws of physics and gravity are questioned." To me, it's a good reason to drive through the redwoods, and the price is right: Tickets are $6 in advance, $5 at the door, but they often sell out during the summer, on holidays, and weekends. Children three years of age and under get in free. Parking is $5. The bumper stickers cost $1.

28

Travel

Air

Hipmonk.com may be the easiest airfare-booking site online. Input just the bare amount of information — where you want to go and when — and Hipmonk offers a series of grids that display your choices across multiple airlines. You can choose by price, flight duration, or arrival or departure time. Hipmonk then ranks each flight by your criteria. If you have multiple concerns, Hipmonk has you covered with a grid that measures agony; i.e., price, duration, and number of stops.

Kayak.com offers up the most reasonable way to find the best deal available for a flight. First it asks you where you want to go and then shows you what's available at that moment. Then you sign up for weekly updates on price and, if you wish, an alert that keeps track of specific destinations and lets you know each time a price drops. On a recent trip to Ireland, Kayak saved me $500 per ticket.

SeatGuru.com is a website that makes sure you get the most out of your airline dollar by showing you exactly what you're buying. It color-codes the seats so you know which ones are best and how much room they offer you. If comfort while traveling is important to you, this is your website.

Lodging

AirBnB.com has a place to stay for everyone. Want to go on the cheap and just need a bedroom in a family home on the outskirts of town? AirBnB has you covered. If you want a first-rate beach house all to yourself, AirBnB has that, too. This is like match.com for vacations, linking up those with a room or house to rent with those who need a room or house.

CouchSurfing.com is for those who don't need a room, or even a bed, just a place to crash. Sure, a bed and room might be had, but those who really make this work are willing to sleep just about anywhere. If you have a couch you can be a host.

GetARoom.com looks like your average online hotel room-booking site, but it offers so much more. The prices listed are really just the starting point. A toll-free phone number listed with the price allows you to call a reservation agent and get an even better deal. Why do it this way? Hotels don't let resellers publish rates below a certain level. GetARoom gets around that by publishing the lowest allowed rate, then "telling" you the actual best rate over the phone.

HomeExchange.com – If you're willing to swap your home with another family, you can save a great deal on vacations. Most homes in the Bay Area are desirable, so exchanging your home for a place at the beach in France is often a piece of cake.

Venere.com is a site that offers accommodations worldwide. In Europe travelers swear by it. Family travelers depend on it when booking rooms in Europe. Most European travel is based on single or double rooms; those looking for a room that can accommodate a family find there's little out there. This site finds the best and cheapest for families of four and five.

VRBO.com (Vacation Rentals by Owner) is the big dog in this field. Those with a home to rent out are matched up with those who want to rent a home.

Rental Cars

AutoSlash.com checks for coupons and codes that will bring down the price of your rental. Then, after you book, it keeps track of the rental: if the price drops, it rebooks your rental at the lower price, and then sends you an email telling you about the new deal. As of this writing, the big-name rental car companies are no longer participating. Things could change, so double-check before booking.

RentalCarMomma.com and **RentalCodes.com** are two good starting points for finding discount codes for rental cars. RentalCarMomma is one of the most user-friendly sites, and RentalCodes is about the most direct.

Cruises

CruiseCompete.com is where travel agents compete for your business. Instead of you bidding on a vacation, hundreds of travel agents bid for your cruise dollars. The site also features a searchable database of cruise deals.

CruiseCritic.com has an amazing array of information on cruising. The COMPARE CRUISE function is a real money saver.

FreighterCruises.com is a website devoted to cruises on non-cruise ships. This is a unique way to see the world, and this site is a good starting point for investigating the possibilities.

Food and Entertainment

Entertainment.com is the fundraising book that offers thousands of dollars in discounts for restaurants, attractions, and shopping. Buy the book specific to your vacation destination, and you'll save some serious money on meals and entertainment. The books cost $30 and come with a mobile app.

Restaurant.com is always a good deal, offering half-price meals; however, if you sign up for email notifications, the meals are almost free. A $25 certificate for a restaurant is often sold for just $2. Read the fine print, look for restaurants in your vacation destination, and you'll save plenty.

Other

BeatOfHawaii.com is the place to go if you love Hawaii and good deals. This site lists cheap flights to the islands, cruises, and hotel rooms that start in the double digits, not the triple ones. Great travel tips as well.

Hotwire.com and **Priceline.com** are wonderful websites for those willing to really go for a deal. It takes some work to get the very best out of these sites, but those who put in the effort to go online, find the latest bidding strategies, and then make multiple bids do extremely well. Both sites also offer non-bid pricing.

InsureMyTrip.com is a comparison site for travel insurance. More than twenty major insurance companies are represented here.

LasVegasAdvisor.com is where the insiders go for information on everything Vegas. Half off of shows is just the starting point. It also offers advice on which casinos offer the best odds.

Vegas.com is for those who really want to get the most out of their trip to sin city. The best part of this website is the nightlife section where you can front-of-the-line passes for the hottest clubs in town.

29

Other

The Packaging Store

Address	1255 Howard Street San Francisco, CA 94103
Phone	415 558-8100
Website	www.the-packaging-store.com
Days & hours of operation	Mon.–Fri. 8:30 AM–5:30 PM Sat. 10 AM–5 PM

Description

Also in Santa Clara

Say you need a box for moving, to ship something cross-country, or to pack up a gift for a friend. This huge warehouse is your one-stop shop for all of that. They have all the packing materials and cardboard boxes in any size you could need, plus gift-wrap, tissue paper, and corrugated boxes for small gifts in every size imaginable. You'll find boxes and bags in odd shapes that can hold two wine bottles, and organza gift bags in various sizes and colors for jewelry. They offer an array of reusable totes, made from recyclable materials, for lugging groceries around. They sell for about $1.50. Prices on all the boxes vary depending on how many you buy. You'll save about 50% if you buy in large quantities. Gift boxes in various colors, roughly the size of a lunchbox, are about 86 cents each, but if you buy a hundred or more, the price drops to 51 cents. The organza gift bags, perfect for people who make and sell costume jewelry, go for 72 cents, but the price drops to 41 cents if you buy them in quantities over 500. Their selection is vast. If you need a box, no matter what size, you'll find it here.

U.S. Nails Supply

Address	2549 S. King Road, Suite A10 San Jose, CA 95122
Phone	408 274-3862
Website	No working website found.
Days & hours of operation	Mon.–Thurs. 9 AM–7 PM Fri. 9 AM–3 PM Sun. 9 AM–7:30 PM

Description

The store may not be pretty on the outside, but the prices you'll find inside make it worth a stop. It's a beauty-supply store for nails, featuring everything you'll need for your next home manicure. They carry thousands of bottles of nail polish, in every color imaginable. They offer name brands like OPI, Essie, and China Glaze — and at good prices. Nail polish sells for $4–$4.75 a bottle, about half what you'd pay elsewhere, with better deals the more you buy. Get ten, for example, and your price on some brands drops to $2.75 each. You can get lots of other nail supplies, too, like packages of eighty emery boards for $12, nail art for $1.50, and commercial-style nail dryers for $60. I also saw huge bottles of nail-strengthening Hoof Lacquer for $6. If nails are your thing, this could be your new favorite store.

Did We Miss a Store?

If your favorite store isn't in this book, what should you do? Tell me about it. The Bay Area retailing landscape is huge, and perhaps I've never heard of your special favorite. Photocopy the form below, fill it out, and mail it to me at the address on the next page. Convince me that I should include it when I update this book or write another.

Store Name: _____

Address: _____

_____

City: _____ CA

Zip code: _____

Phone: _____

Email: _____

Why it should be included:

How do you know about this retailer?

Money-Back Guarantee

I want you to love this book so much you'd marry it, so keep it for 180 days; then, if you want a divorce, okay, I will give you the price of the book back.

The book must be returned with the original receipt. Duh!

This offer is good for two years from the publication date of this book. After that you're on your own.

I will return the price you paid for the book up to the retail price printed on the cover of the book, plus sales tax. No refund for shipping or any other expense.

Easy-beezy: Just send the book, the original receipt, and your name and address to:

Wires & Lights Publishing
3000 F Danville Blvd., #219
Alamo, CA 94507

Index

C

F

G